THE CAT LOVER'S COOKBOOK

JANE MORIN SNOWDAY

J. N. TOWNSEND PUBLISHING

Tivoli, New York

The text of this book is composed in Bookman Light, with display type set in Serif Gothic.

Composition by Stevens Graphics, Brattleboro, Vermont.

Book and cover design by Martha E. Raines.

Photographs by Dyana VanCampen.

Printed in Hong Kong by South China Printing Company.

First Edition

Library of Congress Cataloging-in-Publication Data
Snowday, Jane Morin.
    The cat lover's cookbook.

    1. Cookery.   I. Title.
TX715.S6763 1987   641.5   87-13445
ISBN 0-9617426-1-5

J. N. Townsend Publishing
P.O. Box 418, Tivoli, New York 12583

Dedication

This book is for Christopher Charles Collins, my first born, and Catherine Victoria Collins Stratton, my last born, both of whom, in spite of all those too-hard soft-boiled eggs, too-soft scrambled eggs, and the unsoft fried eggs (funny side up), were a great audience who never let the cook off the hook. Here's to lamb soup, Hostess Twinkies, Beouf en Gelée, The Kumquats, big lumb tapioca, and big man cheese, too.

I appreciate your indulgence while I experimented, and your applause when I was successful. And I recognize that it is both a compliment and a critique that the two of you have grown up to be good cooks. For both of which, I thank you.

C o n t e n t s

Desserts *(continued)*

INTRODUCTION

Beware of people who don't like cats.
—Irish proverb

Those of us who love cats know why — those who don't, don't. There's no point in trying to explain to non-cat people why we love these self-sufficient, aloof, ornery, independent, finicky, furry creatures. Besides, cats have claws, and very sharp teeth, and they kill and sometimes even eat birds. Beautiful, singing, soaring birds — and skittery little mice, too.

The fluid grace of an all black cat as he walks through a broad splash of sunlight on his way to his chosen sleeping spot does not excite the un-catted. Nor are they delighted by the leaps and rolls and purposeless chases of a three-month-old kitten just becoming aware of his own potential. "They" think cats are aloof, and they are correct. Cats are, to those who are.

But cats who are held close in the comforting curve of a friend's arm, who are stroked from their fine-boned faces along a malleable and responsive backbone to the tip of a slowly flexing tail, whose mysterious eyes are peered into with admiration and wonder — these cats are lovers.

And like all lovers they always want *more*—more hugs, more strokes, more kisses.

And more food.

Because my cats are so serious about their meals, it seemed natural to write a cookbook for other cat lovers who enjoy the good company of cats, and good food, and who do not feel a cat in the kitchen is uncouth.

I believe that when you love someone, you tend to like the things they like, and you try to do your best for them. I love my cats. My two and the four before them have always been my friends and have loved me back. A cat cannot be conned. He is totally devoted to his own good, first and foremost. If you help him find contentment, if you feed, shelter, and protect him, he will return your love with the same unconditional love he has for himself.

I have always felt that planning, cooking and serving a truly good meal to someone you love is a loving act. You insult others when you don't give them your best, whether you're working with them, serving a meal, or loving them. We humans have a lot to learn from cats, who always expect the best from themselves and their companions.

My two cats, black Sidney Snowday Boy Cat, and Miss Blue (named after the song "Little Girl Blue"), a Siamese Sealpoint, get fed breakfast before anyone else in the house, including guests, because they are madly insistent and of single purpose. They meet just outside my bedroom door when I emerge at dawn. Miss Blue starts with a long, low sound that slowly reaches the higher registers of cat queries and always sounds like "How can you be so uncaring and selfish and when will you ever change?" If I were more musical, I could tell the key at which she starts this reproachful crescendo and the high note on which she ends it; but whatever it is, its effect on the autonomic nervous system is such that I hurry downstairs to the bathroom, hesitant even to take the time to brush my teeth.

Black Sidney, larger, longer, and sleeker by about one-third than Miss Blue, leaps off the banister and rushes down the steps after me making monotonous meows, rhythmically spaced as if he had his own built-in miniature metronome. Surrounded by Miss Blue's wailing and Sidney's moaning, I emerge as quickly as I can from the bathroom and race to the kitchen. There Sidney heightens his decibel level and begins jumping up and down from the floor to the counter where the electric can opener stands. When I turn to the cupboard containing cat food he rushes that too. As I turn toward the can opener, can in hand, he rushes both. In the interest of his safety, I cannot permit him to keep his nose on the ever enlarging aperture around the rim of the can as it is opened. Cats' noses are very tender and they tear easily on tin, but does Sidney know that? Or care? Every day for the last nine years he's done his great leaping demonstration up to the can opener and down to the floor while I hold the can to the cutting edge with one hand and deflect him from it with the other. Of course, I feed him first. Always.

Miss Blue sits quietly on the counter throughout all of this watching with that contented patience of a creature who knows exactly what is coming her way. She will eat from her saucer placed conveniently on the counter, out of any drafts and away from the roving eye and omnivorous mouth of Sidney Snowday. Miss Blue eats half as much as Sid and takes twice as long to do so, but she does it so delicately that she is a delight to watch. As Sidney hunches over his saucer as if to hide it from hordes of ravening cats that might be racing toward his food, Miss Blue chooses each bite carefully and seems to savor every flavor.

After their meals, they leave their feeding spots with looks of fulfillment, find a pleasant area, preferably in sunlight, and indulge in that activity unique to felines — cleaning. Sidney and Miss Blue carefully wash their whiskers, faces, legs, feet (even between the toes), backs, ears, etc. Then like all the world's creatures who have fed finely and fully, they fall deeply to sleep.

Obviously, food is important to cats, as it is to humans and other creatures. Taken out of the wild, cats are dependent upon us to give them food to live on and to enjoy. I have heard that a mouse is the ideal food for a cat; it has the right amount of minerals, protein, fat, and roughage a cat requires to thrive. I will not, however, keep a mouse farm in the basement to feed my cats. In fact, my cats thrive on canned food, as most do. Yet I find myself cooking foods with ingredients they like. I didn't plan it that way, nor did I recognize the fact until one day I noticed that when I cook, my cats stand at attention. Each has a spot

*Sidney posing in front of his painting, Sidney in Soho, acrylic on burlap,
by Michael Lawrence, 1980.*

from which to attend me: Sidney, on the narrow stretch of counter edging
the stove, Miss Blue on top of the old KLH radio that is constantly tuned to
National Public Radio and sits at the farthest edge of the preparation counter of
my cooking island. They sit and watch. Sometimes they comment when a particularly succulent piece of liver or fish comes into view, or when I'm slicing
freshly poached chicken breasts. Their comments are polite requests for a taste,
which I grant, of course. But then they look at me as if to say, "A little more,
please, would be welcome." Since my business at the time is cooking, I don't
encourage them too much. If I should foolishly leave the site unattended, even
for a moment, Sidney would have the chicken breast on the floor in a flash. He
wouldn't eat it all — just what he wanted at the time. The rest could be mine.

  I cook a lot. While I worked as a copywriter, editor and/or creative director of
an advertising agency, I planned and cooked two meals a day for twenty-five
years as a wife and mother. I also cooked most of the meals in my family's house
in Pittsburgh from the time I was about twelve until I left home at age nineteen.
My father would promise to pay the going restaurant or bakery price of any
dessert or entrée I created that he deemed equal to commercial standards. I
didn't get much allowance and those five dollar bills he gave me (I grew up
during the latter years of the depression) seemed a fortune. So I assiduously
studied the only cookbook we had in the house, *The Mystery Chef Cookbook*, to
find recipes I could handle on the budget he set for me. My father's payment-
incentive plan was certainly the original stimulus for getting me to the stove,
but throughout my childhood, whenever I cooked a meal for him, his words of
approval encouraged and pleased me.
  I understood that Father knew about good food and how to serve it. He
learned from *his* father. He always touched a dinner plate when it was placed
before him to test its temperature. If it was not hot, back it went. He'd explain to
me, "Your grandfather taught me that. Never put hot food on a cold plate." Cold
drinks — beer, martinis, champagne, white wine — must be served in chilled
glasses. And, he said, when serving a baked potato, one should never open it
with a knife. "It destroys the flakiness and seals out the butter," he explained.
Also, bananas must not be cut with a knife if they are to be served with cream
or as part of a dessert. "Break them, my dear, break them in pieces. The metal
spoils the flavor."
  I have always followed his advice as peculiar as it sometimes has seemed
because I've found that those particular foods always taste better when I do.
One time, while observing me tearing apart a banana with my fingers, he
nodded approvingly and said, "Three generations of cranks. Well, it's nobody's
business and we enjoy it, don't we?" You're right, Father, we do. Thank you.

Today I am glad for that experience because cooking truly gives me pleasure. I like everything about it; the shapes and colors of the fruits and vegetables I find startlingly beautiful. I enjoy handling them and washing them and even peeling and slicing them (I think I like that part a little better since my late husband, Mike, bought me one of the first Cuisinarts about eleven years ago). I like the smells, the aroma of young scallions and minced garlic as they are lightly sautéed in butter. Standing by the stove, awaiting the exact moment to add fresh ripe tomatoes to the scallions, and a bit of minced garlic, some pitted black Greek olives, and a handful of fresh basil strips all to become a light delicious sauce for pasta, I am delighted.

The best thing about cats and food is that they like all the best ingredients, not those found in *nouvelle cuisine*, but cream, butter, soft cheeses, poultry, fish, shrimp, scallops (Sidney's predecessor, Leo, once ate two pounds of scallops I had marinating for seviche).

Cats also love liver, of which they get a lot in my kitchen. For years I made twelve pounds of chicken and calves liver paté for end-of-year holiday parties. Each year that day produced lots of bits and pieces for my kitties to enjoy.

Cats love kidneys too. And while my children were young I made many an Irish kidney stew from my grandmother Morin's recipe as well as Veal Kidney Flambé for special guests and buffets.

My friends call me a casual cook because I don't stand over bowls measuring exactly and because I can carry on a conversation while putting together some recipes I've done often, or that I'm inventing as I go. But I do have many favorite recipes that require close reading and careful measuring, such as the four-page recipe for Coulibiac that my daughter Cass and I have been making for Easter for the last few years. Obviously, that is not a dish to attempt when I have guests who want to converse while I fix dinner. But you should see how the cats make out during the salmon and vegetable interlaying part of the preparation!

I like my cats to watch me cook. Being there with me, they remind me of their love of pleasure, good food, and comfort. So what you will find on the pages that follow is a selection of recipes made with the foods cats like best. These recipes are all for people but cats will like a taste, if you please. Some of these recipes are simple and take little time to prepare, but they're good and satisfying. Others will take more time and are worth every minute.

You will find a lot of what we used to call "security foods" in this book — custards, puddings, soufflés, creamy sauces — as well as saucy chicken, duck, quail, kidneys, and liver. I hope you like them, as do Sidney and Miss Blue. So please turn the page and explore the various <u>cat</u>egories of foods put together by a cat lover who loves to cook.

Satchmo, a member of the J. N. Townsend Publishing staff,
caught with his whiskers in the whipped cream.

C R E A M

He who denies the cat milk must give the mouse cream.
—French proverb

Things are seldom what they seem,
Skim milk masquerades as cream.
—Gilbert, *HMS Pinafore*, Act I

The first time I realized just how different cream was from milk was a cold January day when I was told to bring in the two quarts of milk left at our back door by Mr. Bell, the milkman. The sight of that tower of yellow cream that had been pushed up through the fluted paper bottle top by the bluish white frozen milk surprised me. I saw then that cream was very different from milk. I touched it and could feel the butterfat. Even cold as it was, it looked more appetizing. Then my mother cut the cream off the top of the bottle with a butter knife and put it aside, saying "That's for your father's coffee." I guess she had always saved the cream for him but until I saw it high above the milk I hadn't realized what I was missing. That day I think I began to realize the benefits of age, rank, and privilege. If I had heard the line quoted above from Gilbert and Sullivan's *HMS Pinafore*, I would have thought it quite silly. Clearly cream had it all over skim milk — it was smooth and had a rich, luxurious taste and it coated the spoon and made even shredded wheat taste like something besides straw.

Soon homogenized milk was introduced and that was the end of Father's cream. As it happened, my parents separated soon afterwards, and I knew there would be little cream in any form from then on.

When I had my own household, however modest, I bought cream by the half-pintful — heavy cream too — not to use lavishly but for special dishes such as strawberry shortcake, banana pudding, or my daughter's favorite, tapioca, or apple crisp. My children knew early on that there was cream to be had.

And my cats knew too. Their exquisitely fine-tuned olfactory senses are uncanny sometimes. If I'm fixing salted, thinly sliced cucumbers with a sauce of vinegar, water, dill and a little sugar, my cats do not appear at their watching posts by the stove and the kitchen radio. But let me decide to add some cream to the dressing for the cucumbers, and two deeply sleeping cats arise from the darkest corners of the closet or sofa they've chosen as napping places and saunter nonchalantly into the kitchen, stretching as they emit loud, questioning meows and flick their tails impatiently. Sidney is the most impatient of the two and jumps immediately up to the counter where the cream container is sitting open. Knowing that he will put his paw into the container the second he is close enough to it, I pour what I need into a narrow-necked bottle I keep just for such occasions and whisk the container into the refrigerator. Sometimes I'm not quick enough, and the black paw is into the cream and into his mouth before I can stop him. Then what do I do with a half-pint of paw-dipped cream? Empty it down the sink? Horrors! It was 93 cents a half pint the last time I bought it. Do I pour a little into each of their dishes and give them the treat they came for and label the container "Cat's Cream" and refrigerate it until the next time they come crying for cream? Of course I do.

Today cream is eschewed by most authorities on nutrition and by young cooks, including my son and daughter, both good cooks, because it's fattening and loaded with cholesterol. They are all quite right, I'm sure, and quite thin, and more disciplined in matters of food than I. Like my cats, I believe cream has an important place in cooking and shouldn't be substituted. Use less of it, certainly, but enjoy it when it's called for. While researching cream for this chapter, I came across the following in a 1925 edition of Fannie Farmer's *The Boston Cooking-School Cook Book*: "Among fats cream and butter are of first importance as foods, on account of their easy assimilation." There probably have been twenty later editions of that book since 1925, but when it comes to butter and cream, I believe that one.

One of the best things about cream is the way you can easily alter its consistency and flavor; you can change common cream to Devonshire cream for topping berries and other fruits just by heating it slowly to a temperature of about 150 degrees F. When I was a child the cream didn't always whip, but of course today you can easily whip cream to high peaks with an electric beater or a food processor attachment (just be certain the beaters and the cream are very cold). And you can easily make Crème Fraîche by adding two teaspoons of buttermilk to a half pint of sweet heavy cream and letting it sit out for twenty-four hours.

I find that cream has opened a new chapter in the pleasure of pasta dining, and so I've included several versions of these cream sauces for pasta below, and lots of other ways to add the flavor and richness of cream to eggs, vegetables, chicken and desserts. Just remember, don't cook with cream every day or even every week, but if you need to balance a highly flavored entrée with something soothing, think of cream. Your cat will be glad of it and so will you.

Cream Sauces for Pasta

Sauces for pasta made with cream are, to my mind, about the best things to happen to American cuisine, or should I say Italian–American cuisine, since the GIs brought home new tastes after World War II. Most of the dishes here I've enjoyed in the homes of friends and one or two I have developed myself and tried them out on friends. Should I tell you which? Read on and let me know.

First of all, I have to say that I don't make my own pasta because I've been spoiled by living for many years just a few blocks away from Raffetto's Italian Pasta Store on West Houston Street in New York City. I discovered Raffetto's when we first moved to Soho because my daughter, Cass, loved ravioli more than life. So I decided to serve several kinds of ravioli with two different sauces at a party for her twenty-first birthday. I bought a box of spinach and cheese raviolis to test their quality and made a little sauce of garlic and oil and Parmesan. The ravioli were excellent, tender, well-flavored and what a difference freshness made! So I ordered 500 for Cass's party and believe me, the fame of Raffetto's spread that night. I like to think my white clam sauce and red Marinara sauce had something to do with our guests' enjoyment, but I know it's the pasta that makes the difference and a good sauce can't disguise a poor pasta. So, if you can't buy fresh pasta nearby, then I have to say to make your own. Lots of my friends do that, and now that I have to carry my pasta supply from Houston Street up to the Hudson Valley in New York State, I may join them.

How to Cook Pasta:

Among cooks there is some disagreement about the amount of water required to cook one pound of pasta. A famous cook from Italy, Jean Govoni Salvadore says in her good book, *Cooking Ideas from Villa d'Este*, to use seven to eight quarts of boiling water for one pound of pasta. That's three or four more than I use. Some friends of mine always use five quarts of water. So you can see there is some latitude in this matter of how to properly cook pasta. All I can honestly say is, use at least four quarts and more if you like, but don't exceed Senora Salvadore's recommendaton.

Add two tablespoons vegetable oil after the water boils and stir well (you can use olive oil instead). Add pasta and stir again to keep it from sticking. I've suggested earlier to cook pasta al dente. Having written that phrase so many times, I realize that I should say something about what al dente means. It's difficult to say how long one should let the pasta boil to reach the desired state. It can be from seconds to 10 minutes depending on whether it is homemade or not, the size of the pasta, and the brand. There is only one sure way to tell and that's obvious: bite it. Usually when the pasta comes to the top of the water it is ready to be drained and immediately sauced. All the pasta recipes in this book call for one pound of pasta, which serves four as an entrée or six as an appetizer.

Note also that freshly grated Parmesan (there is no substitute for it!) is always called for with cream, meat, and vegetable pasta sauces. It is not mentioned for fish pasta dishes (except for those with anchovies) because the Parmesan's strong flavor kills the delicate flavor of the fish. So garnish your fish pasta sauces with finely minced fresh parsley or a few leaves of fresh basil, cut or torn into strips.

Remember, there are thirty-two kinds of pasta. This book gives you recipes for only about one-fourth of them. So after finding out those you like, try experimenting with others. Pasta cream sauces are so easy to make they invite you to invent your own combinations of flavors, textures, and colors. And really, the only limitation is what *you* like.

Miss Blue loves a snooze on the warm surface of the stove.

Two Cream Sauces for Ravioli

How to Cook the Ravioli:

Both of these recipes are for fresh ravioli stuffed with spinach and cheese because I prefer those to meat or plain cheese ravioli. The first recipe with fresh mushrooms and cream, would be good over meat ravioli. Experiment and decide what you prefer. The fresh ravioli cook quickly so start testing them a minute or two after they rise to the surface of the boiling water. It takes four quarts of water to cook one pound of ravioli. Because I'm watching my salt intake, I don't add salt to the water, although lots of cooks do. But you should add a couple of tablespoons of vegetable oil to keep fresh pasta from sticking. All recipes are for 1 pound of pasta. (See page 9 for more information on cooking pasta.)

Mushrooms, Parmesan, and Cream

4 ounces fresh mushrooms
4 tablespoons butter
1 cup heavy cream
1/4 cup grated Parmesan
Freshly ground black pepper
3 tablespoons finely chopped
   parsley

After washing the mushrooms, trim the stems, separate from caps and slice stems lengthwise. I always wash them in cold water and dry them with a paper towel before I sautée them very lightly in the melted butter. If caps are large, slice them into 1/4-inch pieces and toss them into the skillet where you have melted the 3 tablespoons of butter. Stir them around to coat them with butter and cook about one minute. Remove mushrooms with slotted spoon so that most of the butter stays in the skillet, and place on a warm plate. Keep warm.

Add another tablespoon of butter to skillet, melt it, then add cream and bring sauce just to boiling point, add Parmesan, stir it in quickly, remove from heat and add the lightly cooked mushrooms. Coat them with sauce, add the parsley. Put the cooked ravioli in a warm bowl and toss gently. Serve with all-important bowl of freshly grated Parmesan on the table. The freshly ground pepper is added to individual taste as well.

Anchovies, Parmesan, and Cream

2 tablespoons butter
8 anchovy fillets, sliced
   lengthwise
1 large clove garlic, mashed
   with broad side of heavy
   knife
1 cup heavy cream
1/2 cup freshly grated
   Parmesan
Freshly ground black pepper

Melt the butter in a skillet, add the mashed garlic, stir it around until it softens and separates, then add the anchovies. Cook them until they're mushy—it only takes a couple of minutes. Add the cream, bring to just boiling point, stirring occasionally while it simmers for a few minutes. Add Parmesan and cook until it thickens. I arrange the cooked ravioli on a hot plate and sauce generously to serve. A garnish of black Italian olives with pepper and a few julienne strips of sweet red peppers make an attractive presentation. Put the bowl of Parmesan and the pepper mill on the table.

Three Cream Sauces for Fettuccine

How to Cook Fettuccine:

Put four quarts of water into a large pot. Put one teaspoon of salt and a couple tablespoons of vegetable oil in the water after it has reached a boil. Add the fettuccine to the boiling water and cook until al dente. Drain thoroughly because you don't want even a drop of water clinging to the pasta that will dilute the delicious cream sauce. Remember, have the sauce just about ready when you put the pasta into the boiling water because you'll only have about 8 minutes to finish up the sauce while the pasta cooks al dente.

If you must use dried fettuccine, follow package directions and accommodate the sauce preparation to the time allowed. All recipes are for 1 pound of pasta.

Peas, Sicilian Olives, Julienne Red Pepper, and Cream

5 tablespoons butter
1 cup heavy cream
1 cup frozen peas
1/2 cup freshly grated
   Parmesan
1/4 cup Sicilian Olives, pitted
   and halved
1/2 large sweet red pepper,
   seeded and cut by hand
   into thin Julienne strips

Use a medium skillet, put half the butter to melt, add the heavy cream and bring just to a boil. Cook, stirring occasionally, about five minutes. Turn off the heat, stir in the Parmesan, add the frozen peas, the olives, and put over low heat to keep warm but not to boil. When the pasta is drained, toss it with the remaining softened butter in a large heated bowl. Add the strips of red pepper and stir them in just before you add the hot cream sauce. Remember to heat your serving bowls. And put a generous bowl of freshly grated Parmesan on the table.

Fresh Asparagus, Ham, Parmesan, and Cream

3 tablespoons butter
2 tablespoons minced
  scallions
2 cloves of garlic, minced
1 pound asparagus as young
  and thin as possible
1/3 cup ham,* cut in thin
  slivers
1 cup heavy cream
1/2 cup freshly grated
  Parmesan
Freshly ground black pepper

Cook the asparagus in about four cups of boiling water in a skillet big enough to accommodate their length (trim the tough ends). Cook until just tender and drain. Cut the tips off, put aside. Cut the stalks in half (lengthwise) and cut again into inch and a half lengths.

Melt butter in a skillet over moderate heat and cook the scallions until soft. Add ham and garlic; cook until garlic is soft. Add the asparagus pieces, stir into the butter mixture, then add the cream, stirring over moderately high heat. Add the freshly grated Parmesan and toss mixture into the hot buttered fettuccine in a warm serving bowl. Add salt and pepper to taste.

*If you can get the Italian ham, prosciutto, at an Italian grocery in your neighborhood, try this recipe with it. The flavor is different and delicious.

Parmesan, Fresh Basil, and Cream

4 tablespoons butter
1 cup heavy cream
3/4 cup freshly grated
  Parmesan
1/2 cup fresh basil leaves,
  cut in strips

Melt half the butter in a medium skillet, add the heavy cream and bring to a simmer. Cook about six minutes until cream is thickened. Stir the Parmesan until the sauce thickens; add the strips of fresh basil. After tossing the pasta with the remaining butter, add the sauce and toss again. Remember the heated serving bowls and freshly grated Parmesan to add to taste. And put the pepper mill on the table, too.

Cream Sauce for Lobster Newburg

1/2 stick butter
6 tablespoons flour
1 pint cream
1 pint milk
1 pint evaporated milk
1 1/2 teaspoons salt
1/2 teaspoon freshly ground
   black pepper
1/4 teaspoon nutmeg
1/2 cup sherry
1/2 cup fresh mushrooms,
   chopped

Melt the butter in a saucepan, remove from the fire and stir in the flour; mix it well with the butter, and add the cream a little at a time at first, stirring constantly. Then add the milk and evaporated milk. Return to the fire and cook slowly, stirring all the time. Add salt and pepper, nutmeg, sherry and mushrooms. Keep cooking and stirring and scraping the bottom (to prevent scorching) until it thickens. Makes 8 cups for 8 servings.

How to Cook the Lobster with the Sauce
(two servings at a time):
1/4 stick butter
2 cups lobster meat chunks
2 tablespoons brandy
2 cups Newburg sauce
Toast triangles
Rice

Don't try to cook over two helpings of lobster Newburg at a time.

Melt the butter in a skillet and add the lobster meat chunks and brandy. Flame the brandy. Sautée gently until the meats are lightly cooked. Add 2 cups of the Newburg sauce and cook for 3 or 4 minutes longer, stirring carefully so as not to break up the lobster chunks. Serve it in individual casserole dishes with rice on the side and a good white wine.

Chicken Mousse with Cream

1 cup chicken, cut finely
1 cup well seasoned stock
2 egg yolks, well beaten
1/2 teaspoon cayenne pepper
1 tablespoon gelatin
1 cup whipped cream
3 egg whites
Salt to taste

Combine first five ingredients, bring to a simmer enough to cook yolks. Cool. Add gelatin soaked in 1/4 cup of cold water and dissolved in a little hot water, then the whipped cream, egg whites (beaten dry) and salt. Beat well. Pour into mold. Chill until firm.

Serve on a bed of mixed greens with a few slivers of fresh red pepper (sweet) for color. For a dressing, I'd thin some homemade mayonnaise with a little sweet cream and lemon or lime juice. Mix well, taste. Don't overdo the juice. Start with a tablespoon to one cup of thinned mayonnaise and increase if you like a tarter dressing. You can also add a teaspoon of fresh chopped chervil or dill if you like. This makes a nice summer luncheon or buffet dish and this recipe will serve four nicely with a little hot bread and some fresh vegetable garnish.

Sour Cream Dressing

2/3 cup thick sour cream
1 teaspoon salt, or more to
   taste
2 tablespoons catsup
   (optional)
Sugar to taste
   (about 1 level tablespoon)
Dash Tabasco sauce
Juice 1 lemon or
   mild vinegar to taste
1 to 1 1/2 teaspoons
   prepared mustard
1 tablespoon chopped chives,
   parsley, or chervil

Mix the cream with the salt, Tabasco, lemon juice, catsup (optional), and prepared Dijon mustard. Add chives, parsley, or chervil. Pour over the salad and mix well. Add sugar to taste.

Paprika Mushrooms with Cream

4 tablespoons butter
1 pound mushrooms
1 tablespoon Worchester-
   shire sauce
1 tablespoon flour
1 cup chicken broth or
   sweetbread broth
1/2 cup milk
1/2 cup cream
1 teaspoon paprika
Salt, pepper to taste

Brown butter in a skillet. Add mushrooms (caps separated from trimmed stems), salt and pepper. Cover, simmer until mushrooms are done—10 minutes. Stir occasionally. Add milk mixed with flour, and all other ingredients. Cook until thickened. Serve over noodles or rice.

Cream Corn Pones

1 cup unsifted white corn
  meal
1/2 teaspoon salt
1/4 cup thick sweet cream
1 tablespoon melted lard for
  skillet
1/2 cup boiling water
1 tablespoon melted lard or
  butter
1 teaspoon baking powder

Put corn meal into a bowl. Add salt to meal and stir in the boiling water. The mixture will resemble dry crumbs. Cover the bowl and set in the refrigerator an hour or so to chill. Just before you are ready to make your pones, bring out your corn meal mixture. Be sure that your oven is hot by this time—450 degrees is about right. Add to meal mixture the 1 tablespoon of melted lard or butter, and baking powder mixed with sweet cream. Stir well. The mixture should be a paste, firm enough to handle. Take heaping tablespoons of this paste and form croquette-like shapes and place in a preheated iron skillet in which there is another tablespoon of melted lard or butter. Then pat the tops with your fingers to flatten them slightly. Put pones in moderate oven and leave them there for half an hour, by this time they should be brown and cooked on the inside. If not, turn them over and let them stay in an extra 5 minutes. Serve them piping hot with beans or greens or soup or salad, and allow at least two to each person. As with biscuits, you always butter while hot. Your feline friends would like a bit of this, too.

Lulu, a love of a cat, belonging to my neighbors, takes a lick of milk while trying not to lose a drop.

Dressed Cucumbers

These cucumbers are delicious and don't require oil. What you can do is drain the marinade after a day or so and mix the cucumbers with 1 cup of sour cream or 1 cup of sweet cream which you have soured with 1 tablespoon of lemon juice. Garnish with finely chopped parsley or fresh dill. Cucumbers fixed like this have been served in our family for as long as I remember. To this day whenever I serve them guests say, "Those cucumbers are wonderful!" And they're *so* easy:

2 medium-sized cucumbers, peeled, scored, and sliced thin
6 spring onions, diced
1/2 cup apple cider vinegar
2 tablespoons sugar, or more to taste
2 tablespoons chopped parsley
1/2 cup water
1 1/2 teaspoons salt, or more to taste
1/4 teaspoon black pepper

Mix the pepper, onions, scored cucumbers (I score them by running a sharp table fork from tip to tip of the unpeeled cucumber, making sure the fork cuts deeply into the skin. Then I go to the fine slicing procedure for which one needs a very good, very sharp knife and lots of patience. I've sometimes used the fine slicing blade of the food processor if I'm in a hurry.) Mix the vinegar and water with the vegetables and seasonings, then store in the refrigerator in a glass jar or tight-fitting freezer container for at least 2 hours. Sans the sour cream, these goodies will last a week in the fridge.

Spinach in Cream

3 pounds young tender
   spinach
1 heaping tablespoon butter
1 tablespoon flour
1 tablespoon finely grated
   onion
1/4 cup heavy whipping
   cream
Salt and pepper to taste

Prepare spinach by washing carefully and discarding all tough stems. Put spinach into two cups boiling water; boil 3 minutes. Drain well. Chop coarsely by hand or food processor. In 2-quart saucepan, melt butter, add flour, blend. Add spinach, onion, cream, salt, and pepper. Heat thoroughly and serve immediately. You can use thick sour cream in place of the whipping cream. Serves 6.

Sidney at the kitchen window waiting for today's fowl to appear on the kitchen counter.

F O W L

My cat and I continued to dine a deux. . . . Every few days I prepared
fowl cooked slowly in a mild chablis with, perhaps, a dash of basil for
piquancy. She enjoyed surprise, especially an unexpected herb in a
savory sauce. . . . The objective of our mealtime ritual of tantalizing
tastes was to prolong my cat's life, but I also wanted her to enjoy
living as never before.
            —Irving Townsend, "The Fourth Cat," *Separate Lifetimes*

A chicken in every pot.
            —Herbert Hoover's 1932 campaign slogan

When I was a child, I liked Sunday dinner best when the main course was
chicken. Of course, that was during the era of the political cry, "A chicken in
every pot!" Since politics were important in our family (Grandfather Morin was
a member of the House of Representatives for eight terms) I attached exceptional importance to political slogans and therefore thought chicken dinners
were something special.

My father managed movie theatres for Warner Brothers and Harris Amuse-
ment Co. in those days. Because theatres in Pittsburgh were closed on Sundays,
we were able to enjoy our family Sunday dinners throughout the depression
years, and I remember them as unquestionably the best of the week. Roasted
chicken was my favorite, with or without the good bread or rice stuffing my
mother made. I soon learned that I liked the white meat best. The gravy that
was offered was exceptionally good, although I didn't have much to compare it
with, except the gray glop we were served at the boarding school I was sent to
for one semester. After I started to cook I discovered my mother's secret was
bacon fat. She had added bacon fat to the drippings in the roasting pan before
she added the flour to make what I now know is roux, and somehow the combination (common in Southern cooking and among the Pennsylvania Dutch in
western Pennsylvania) was delicious and, as you can see, memorable.

By the time my children came along, chicken was plentiful and, perhaps
because of Hoover's slogan years before, low-priced. One could buy a generous
quantity and thus get two meals out of one. I liked that because it meant one
less dinner to prepare during the work week. To make chicken dinners interesting to Chris and Cass I experimented with lots of chicken recipes. Most were
successes, such as Country Captain, Chicken Morengo, Broiled Chicken with
Lemon and Dill (which I thought I had invented) and Chicken Paprika. The four
cats we had at the time enjoyed the scraps from all of our chicken dinners.

Then one weekend we had chicken for dinner but not as the main course.
Actually, it was a rooster who became our surprise weekend guest. His name

was Khrushchev. He was the science project of Chris's sixth grade class and one Friday Chris's homeroom teacher asked if anyone could take the great Khrushchev home for the weekend since the room where he was caged was to be painted. The first hand up was Chris's. He was asked if he had to get permission from his parents. "Oh, no! My mother loves animals," he replied.

During a client meeting at about 3:30 that afternoon, Chris called to announce that he had been allowed to bring Khrushchev the rooster home to our apartment on West 111th Street in New York City from Friday afternoon until Monday morning. When I recovered my composure I told him not to tell the neighbors about our guest, to keep the windows closed and put the bird in the cats' room, and confine the cats elsewhere. When I arrived home from work I got to meet Khrushchev and discovered he was so named because he jumped up and down on one leg while letting out ear-shattering crows. I just hoped he wouldn't spoil the quiet of our neighbors' Saturday morning sleep, not to mention my own. The only answer was to make a perch for him in the cats' room and hang dark curtains at the windows so he wouldn't see the sun rise. By the time we all went to bed, the room was light-proof. We gave Khrushchev a big meal of chicken feed so he would sleep well. Then I tried to sleep well. One o'clock, two o'clock, three o'clock . . . finally I dropped off. Promptly at 5:40 Khrushchev let go the loudest cock-a-doodle-doo Manhattan's ever heard. Somehow the door to the powder room had opened and there, in full sight of all who lived on our air shaft, was this giant, dingy-white rooster sitting on the sill, flapping his wings and announcing the sunrise to five floors of shocked and sleepy people.

Before noon we got a notice from the landlord reminding us that keeping live chickens in our apartment was forbidden in our lease and either the rooster went or we went in thirty days. By the time we found acceptable quarters for Mr. K. it was too late to do the week's grocery shopping, and there was nothing in the house but some leftover chicken legs. We sent out for Chinese. A lot of weeks elapsed before chicken was on the menu again.

All of this is by way of telling you that I'm not going to tell you how to roast, fry or broil chicken. Even neophyte cooks can easily broil or roast chicken and almost every major cookbook tells you how, so I'm including instead directions for poaching chicken, which then opens up a lot of saucing options. While researching the best way to poach chicken I discovered that even those bright stars in the culinary firmament, Julia Child and Simone Beck, did not include poaching chicken in the first volume of *Mastering the Art of French Cooking*. No, they saved it for the second volume where they treated it extensively and devoted almost nineteen pages to it. Poaching is the best way to flavor chicken without using fat and much salt which many cooks are avoiding these days. Poached chicken is also always tender and moist. As a result, small slices trimmed from the breast or thigh are always most appreciated by my pair of culinary monitors, Sidney and Miss Blue.

Miss Blue reluctantly accepts the fact that I must cook the chicken before she is allowed a taste.

How to Poach Chicken:

Buy the best quality chicken you can afford, and figure on a 2 1/2 pound cut-up frying chicken serving four people. Wash the chicken under cold running water. I use a large bowl to soak it in first, and then empty it as I run the water over it. It's ready to cook when the water runs clear. Remember, if you prefer all white meat, you can buy chicken breasts (try to get them all the same size, or trim them yourself), but *don't* buy the boneless because the bones and skin add to the flavor. Now that the chicken is freshened by its cold water bath, salt it lightly and put it in an oven-proof pottery or an enameled metal casserole dish with a lid. Add 1 1/2 cups dry white wine and 2 cups chicken stock or canned chicken broth. Some cooks tie up the herbs in cheesecloth but I never do. I believe you get more of their flavor if you let them float around in the broth and wine, and you can always strain the broth later. However you want to do it, add 1/2 teaspoon tarragon, 1 bay leaf, 1/4 teaspoon thyme and 4 large parsley sprigs. Cover the pot and bring the liquid to a *simmer.* Watch it so it will not boil because that toughens the chicken. Taste and add salt lightly. I usually add six or seven peppercorns at this time to keep salt to a minimum.

Cover again and turn the heat down so the broth and wine stay at a slow simmer. You can do this on top of the stove or in a 325-degree oven. The white meat is finished in about 20 minutes; the dark takes 5 minutes more. Test by piercing with fork—the juices should run yellow, never reddish.

The result will be tender pieces of chicken that have kept their shape and are easily removed from the bones and are ready to be sliced, slivered, cubed, even minced, then sauced and garnished in coats of many colors and flavors.

Chicken Tetrazzini

5 pound stewing chicken, cut
  into serving pieces
1 onion studded with 2 cloves
2 stalks celery with leaves
Salt
1/2 bay leaf
1 carrot
3 cups water
Chicken fat or butter
1/4 cup flour
Tabasco sauce
1/2 pound mushrooms, sliced
1 egg yolk, lightly beaten
1 tablespoon dry sherry
3 tablespoons light cream
1 eight-ounce package
  spaghetti
2 tablespoons grated
  Parmesan cheese
1 teaspoon butter
Toasted almonds

In a heavy kettle place the chicken, onion, celery, one tablespoon salt, bay leaf, carrot and three cups water. Bring to a boil, reduce the heat and simmer, covered, until the chicken is tender. Remove the chicken from the broth and let cool. Remove the meat from the bones, discarding skin and bones, or use poaching method (see page 25). Use two 2-1/2 pound fryers for this recipe.

Skim the fat from the top of the broth and place four tablespoons of the fat (or an equal amount of butter) in a saucepan. Add the flour and salt to taste, stirring with a wire whisk until blended. Meanwhile, bring two cups of the strained chicken broth to a boil and add all at once to the fat-flour mixture, stirring vigorously with the whisk until the sauce is thickened and smooth. Season with Tabasco sauce.

In a skillet heat three tablespoons of the remaining fat or butter, add the mushrooms and cook until just tender.

To the sauce add the egg yolk, lightly beaten with a little of the hot sauce and stir in the sherry, cream, chicken and mushrooms. Cook, stirring, until heated through. Do not let boil.

Cook the spaghetti according to package directions. Place alternate layers of spaghetti and sauce with chicken in buttered baking dish. Put freshly ground Parmesan on top of sauce. Place dish in preheated broiler. Add toasted almonds and serve to 6.

Chicken Stuffed with Macaroni

4 pound chicken
1 stalk celery, with leaves
Sprig of parsley
Salt
1/4 cup butter
2 tablespoons flour
1/2 cup white wine
1/2 cup cream
1/8 teaspoon nutmeg
1/4 teaspoon freshly ground
    black pepper
1/2 pound elbow macaroni
Grated Parmesan cheese

Use poaching method described on page 25, or place the whole chicken in a kettle and add water barely to cover. Add the celery stalk, parsley, and a little salt. Bring to a boil, cover and simmer until the chicken is tender. Remove the chicken to a warm platter and keep hot. Strain the stock and reserve one cup.

In a saucepan, melt the butter, add the flour and stir with a wire whisk until blended. Meanwhile, bring the reserved stock and the cream to a boil and add all at once to the butter-flour mixture, stirring vigorously with the whisk until the sauce is thickened and smooth. Season with the nutmeg, one-half teaspoon salt and the pepper.

Preheat oven to hot (400 degrees).

Cook the macaroni in two quarts boiling salted water until tender, about ten minutes. Drain and mix with half the sauce. Stuff the chicken with the mixture, close the opening and truss. Place, breast side up, in a buttered baking dish. Pour the remaining sauce over the top and sprinkle with grated cheese. Bake until the cheese is browned, about 10 minutes. Serves 4.

Chicken Paprika

2 tablespoons butter
1/2 cup chopped onion
1 clove garlic, minced
1 1/2 tablespoons sweet
   Hungarian paprika
   (You can also add hot
   paprika if you like)
1 teaspoon salt
1 tomato, peeled and
   chopped
1 green pepper, seeded and
   chopped
3/4 cup chicken stock
1 three-pound broiler-fryer
   chicken, cut into pieces
1/4 cup flour
1/4 cup light cream
1/2 cup sour cream

In a heavy kettle, heat the butter, add the onion and garlic and sauté until lightly browned. Add the paprika, salt, tomato, green pepper and stock. Cover and cook 10 minutes.

Add the chicken, cover and cook until tender, about 40 minutes. Add the water or additional chicken stock, if necessary, to make one and one-quarter cups broth.

Add the flour blended with the light cream and a little of the hot sauce and cook, stirring, until thickened.

Add the sour cream and cook until heated through. Do not boil. Serve over noodles or rice. Serves 4.

Tarragon Chicken

3 chickens weighing about
   1 3/4 pounds each
Salt and pepper
Salad oil, chicken fat or
   olive oil
2 carrots
1 onion
1 stalk celery
1 sprig each of parsley,
   thyme, and tarragon
2 cups water

Allow 1/2 chicken for each person. Split down the back, salt and pepper and rub with salad oil, chicken fat or olive oil. Set the chickens under the flame to brown until golden-brown.

Place in a casserole, with carrots, onion, celery, parsley, thyme, and tarragon and juice left from the broiling, plus the water. Set in a moderate oven (350 degrees) in a covered roaster and cook until chickens are done, about 1 hour.

How to Make the Sauce:
4 egg yolks
1 tablespoon flour
1 cup chicken broth
2 tablespoons butter
1/2 cup thick cream
1 teaspoon fresh chopped
   tarragon
2 tablespoons chopped
   parsley

Beat the egg yolks with the flour. Add chicken broth and cook in double boiler with the chicken fat or butter until thick. Add cream, tarragon and chopped parsley. Stir while cooking. Arrange chicken on platter; cover lightly with sauce. Serve remainder in sauce boat. Serves 6.

Ducks Garnished with Olives

1 young duck, about 3 pounds
1 clove garlic
1/4 teaspoon powdered
  ginger
1/2 cup sauterne or
  white wine
1 small bunch celery leaves
1 cup flour
1/4 cup butter
Salt and black pepper to taste
1 1/2 cups water
3 tablespoons catsup
1 onion
1 cup sliced black olives

Clean duck and wash well. Crush a clove of garlic with a teaspoon of salt, ginger, and black pepper, then rub mixture on the inside and outside of duck. Wrap in wax paper and let stand overnight in the icebox.

The next morning rub the duck well with softened butter and dust with flour. Brown under the flame. Transfer to a roasting pan.

Place onion and celery in the duck, season again with salt and pepper. Add water, wine and catsup and cook in a covered pan in a moderate oven (375 degrees) until duck becomes tender— 1 1/2 to 2 hours.

Skim off all fat from gravy and add olives. If gravy is too thick, thin with a bit of wine or water. If too thin, add a flour-and-water paste, allowing 1 tablespoon of flour mixed with 3 of water to each cup of broth. Simmer a few moments to blend. Place duck on a platter surrounded with pickled peaches or small baked apples stuffed with chutney.

Baked Quail and Oysters

4 quail
4 teaspoons butter or
  margarine
Flour in which to roll butter
Salt and pepper to taste
4 strips bacon
4 to 8 oysters, depending on
  size
4 tablespoons consommé or
  meat stock made by dissolv-
  ing 1 bouillon cube in 1/4
  cup of water

Wash and clean quail well. Do not split. Salt and pepper the birds inside and out. Put a piece of bacon over the breast of each bird. Wrap around and tie securely with a piece of string—do not use a toothpick.

Put an oyster or two in each bird, filling the cavity. Place birds in a roasting pan, one beside the other. The oven should be moderately hot, about 375 degrees. Add the consommé or meat broth.

Baste the birds (do not cover them) with their own drippings every 15 minutes and cook until they are tender—40 minutes should be enough. Drop into the pan 4 teaspoons of butter or margarine, each teaspoon of which has been rolled in flour until it will not hold any more. Cook 8 minutes longer or until butter melts and flour thickens gravy. Baste the breasts with the sauce. Serve with rice.

Potted Quail

4 tablespoons butter
4 tiny onions, the size of
  walnuts
1 tablespoon flour
1 cup water
1 clove garlic
4 quail
2 tablespoons minced
  parsley
Salt and pepper to taste
1 cup slivered sautéed
  mushrooms cooked in 1
  tablespoon butter
  (optional)

Melt butter in Dutch oven or chicken fryer. Add garlic. Salt and pepper birds and cook until brown all over. Remove to a plate. Discard garlic and add flour. Cook until brown, stirring constantly. Add water, stir until gravy thickens.

Return birds to gravy, cover and simmer until tender (45 minutes to 1 hour), adding more water if necessary. Add tiny onions and continue cooking until al dente. Just before serving, add the parsley and 1 cup of slivered mushrooms, sautéed 5 minutes in 1 tablespoon of butter. Allow one bird per person. Serve with wild rice.

Country Captain

1 chicken, poached according
   to directions on page 25,
   with skin and bones removed, cut into generous,
   evenly sized pieces
4 tablespoons butter
1 red sweet pepper, sliced thin
1 clove garlic, crushed
1 onion, chopped
1 cup water, more if needed
6 peeled fresh ripe tomatoes
   (use canned if not in
   season)
1 tablespoon chopped fresh
   parsley
1/2 teaspoon ground thyme
1/4 pound blanched almonds
3 tablespoons dried currants
1 1/2 teaspoons curry powder
   (see note in chicken curry
   recipe on page 35)
4 slices crisp bacon

To melted butter add pepper, garlic, and onion; cook 5 minutes, stirring constantly. Add water mixed with curry powder, tomatoes, parsley and thyme. Cook slowly for about 20 minutes.

Pour this mixture over the chicken pieces. Cover and cook on low heat until chicken is heated through. Add the almonds, fried in butter to a golden-brown. Add currants. Place chicken pieces on heated serving platter, cover with sauce. Garnish with bacon slices.

Serve with individual dishes of chutney, chopped hardboiled eggs, grated coconut, chopped peanuts, and chopped scallions as garnishes. Serves 4.

Fricassee of Chicken with Herbs

3 cups chicken broth
1 onion studded with 4
   cloves
1 small carrot, diced
3 peppercorns
1 tablespoon chopped chives
2 tablespoons chopped
   parsley
1 teaspoon salt
1/2 bay leaf
2 two-and-a-half pound frying
   chickens, cut into pieces
6 tablespoons flour
6 tablespoons butter
12 small white onions, peeled
   and left whole
1/2 teaspoon rosemary
1/2 teaspoon marjoram
1/4 teaspoon powdered
   saffron
3 tablespoons light cream
2 egg yolks
1 teaspoon lemon juice

In a heavy kettle combine the broth, onion, carrot, peppercorns, chives, parsley, salt and bay leaf. Bring to a boil.

Dredge the chicken pieces in three tablespoons of the flour. In a skillet, heat three tablespoons of the butter, add the chicken and brown on all sides. Add to the simmering broth and cook, covered, over low heat until the chicken is tender, about 45 minutes, or use poached chicken method (page 25).

Remove the chicken pieces to a warm platter and keep hot. Strain the stock, return it to the heat and add the onions. Cover and cook 45 minutes. Remove the onions to the platter and keep hot.

In a heavy saucepan melt the remaining butter, add the remaining flour and stir with a wire whisk until blended. Add the simmering chicken broth all at once to the butter-flour mixture, stirring vigorously with the whisk until the sauce is thickened and smooth. Add the herbs and additional salt to taste.

Combine cream and egg yolks in a small mixing bowl. Add a little of the heated sauce to the egg yolk mixture, then stir into remaining sauce. Cook until sauce thickens but do not allow it to boil. Add the lemon juice, pour over chickens and onions. Serves 6 to 8.

Nasi Goreng

1 chicken poached, according
  to directions on page 25,
  with skin and bones
  removed, cut into generous, evenly sized pieces.
3 cups chicken broth
1 1/2 cups uncooked rice
2 tablespoons oil
1 large onion, chopped (1 cup)
1 clove garlic, crushed
1 teaspoon coriander seeds,
  crushed
1 teaspoon cumin
1/2 teaspoon crushed dried
  red pepper
1/8 teaspoon mace
2 cups raw shrimp
4 ounces boiled ham
1/2 cup salted peanuts,
  chopped
Soy sauce

Sauté rice in oil until golden. Stir in the
chopped onions, garlic and 1/2 teaspoon
salt. Cook until onion is tender but not
brown. Stir in 3 1/2 cups chicken broth,
coriander, cumin, pepper and mace. Heat
to boiling. Cook broth and rice until rice
is tender and broth is almost absorbed.
Stir in chicken, shrimp, ham, and
chopped peanuts. Heat slowly. Serve hot
with more chopped peanuts and best
quality soy sauce. Serves 4.

Chicken Curry

1 two-and-a-half-pound
  poached chicken
  (see page 25)
1 onion, thinly sliced
1 small tart apple, peeled and
  quartered
1 clove garlic, crushed
2 ounces ghee (see below)
2 cardamons
2 cloves
2-inch stick of cinnamon
1 tablespoon of ground
  coriander
1 teaspoon ground tumeric
1/2 teaspoon ground ginger
1/2 teaspoon ground cumin
  seed
1/2 teaspoon or less of
  ground chilies to taste

Sauté apple, onions, garlic, cloves, cardamons, and cinnamon in ghee; do not let the onions brown. When sufficiently cooked add all the other ingredients. Mix well and cook on a low heat for 4 or 5 minutes.

Add sufficient water or chicken stock to form a thick gravy, cover the pan and simmer until thickened. Add a squeeze of lemon juice. Salt to taste. Add chicken meat, removed from bones and sliced in evenly sized pieces. Heat. Serves 4.

Variations:

When individual ingredients, listed above, are not available for the curry sauce, use commercial curry powder. There are many to choose from in specialty stores, from subtly flavored curry to very hot. Season to taste. This sauce can also be used for meat or shrimp.

Ghee, or clarified butter, is made by melting butter and letting it stand until the clear oil separates and rises to the top. Use only the clear butter.

C H E E S E

Never commit yourself to a cheese without having first examined *it.*
—T. S. Eliot

Clifton Fadiman once said that cheese is "milk's leap to immortality," a rather grand description that I have a problem with, for no cheese that's good enough to be called immortal every stays around my house long enough to justify the use of the word.

Cheese has been a favorite of mine ever since childhood when I discovered there was more to it than the cream cheese and olive spread that came in those little juice glasses. I also became enamored with cottage cheese when my sister Eleanor was born and it was prescribed by the pediatrician for her. Because it was specified for her diet, I grew very fond of it.

But cats and cheese? They are quite a match, in fact, at least in my home. Sidney will swallow any nasty tasting medicine or pill if I coat it with cream cheese. A triple cream cheese like Saga Blue drives him mad with desire. If I mix a little grated Cheddar with his canned "Salmon Supreme" breakfast, he rushes more than usual to finish his portion so he can leap to the counter and start on Miss Blue's leftovers. Miss Blue is of the same opinion about cheese, but she never devours anything or finds any food worth leaping for.

Cheese is an important source of protein, for cats and people alike, and is often included in canned cat food. As with any human food, I give cheese treats sparingly lest Miss Blue and Sidney ruin their fine physiques. Mine, on the other hand, can handle it!

There is an almost infinite variety of cheeses available and I've discovered many over the years that have become favorites. During the years I cooked at home after my father left, I included cheese in two meals each week (all the budget allowed). When I discovered the difference real Cheddar cheese made to Friday's macaroni and cheese casserole, and what freshly grated Parmesan (called simply "Italian" in those days) could do for a very basic tomato sauce I was appalled at what we had been missing. I began looking at the variety of cheeses in the big dairy store in downtown Pittsburgh. It was close to our streetcar stop so I had time to peer through the window and wonder at the intriguing names: Stilton, Liederkranz, Limburger, Roquefort, Emmenthal, Gorgonzola. When I began working as a copywriter just after I turned eighteen, I allowed myself a quarter pound of one of those exotic cheeses each payday. It didn't take long for me to realize that Americans didn't have the great cheeses; they had to be imported. I also learned that to be able to enjoy imported cheese, I had to earn more money.

Sidney and Little Girl Blue were both foundlings. Miss Blue was found when she was 3 weeks old abandoned in a New York City apartment building by the children of Mr. and Mrs. Tim Sullivan. Sidney came to me via longtime friend, Nan Braman, who collects strays, alters and innoculates them and finds them good homes. Sidney was found in the kitchen of a New York City French restaurant. He was a skinny, skittish kitten, and a very welcome addition to our little family.

Cheese does magical things to other foods, to sauces in combination with eggs, to soufflés and puddings and tortas (Spanish for pie and much in favor now that Southwestern cuisine has become so well known and appreciated), that the range of its uses can't be presented in one chapter; so, I've chosen cheese recipes with those cat-favored ingredients: cream, butter, fish, and fowl to give you a sampling of how much improved simple food can be when "milk immortalized" is included.

Shirred Eggs with Cheese Sauce

Make two cups sharp cheese sauce with Dijon mustard and a dash of Tabasco sauce (see page 41 for cheese sauce recipe).

Put 1/2 cup of cheese sauce in the bottom of each individual baking dish. Break 2 eggs on top and pour a tablespoon of cream over the eggs.

Bake about 12 minutes in moderate oven until set.

Cheese Puffit

1 cup left-over cooked ham
1 teaspoon chopped onion
3 tablespoons butter
2 slices bread, 1/2 inch thick
1/4 pound Cheddar cheese
2 eggs, separated
1/4 teaspoon paprika
1/2 teaspoon salt
1 1/3 cups hot milk
1 tablespoon parsley, finely
    chopped

Chop ham and onion in food processor, fry gently for 3 minutes with butter. Put in greased baking dish. Crumble bread (crust too) into small pieces, sliver cheese or grate coarsely. Combine bread, cheese, beaten egg yolks and heated milk; add extra tablespoon butter, salt and paprika. Let stand 20 minutes or until ready to bake. Add parsley, then fold in stiffly beaten egg whites. Pour into baking dish over ham. Bake in slow oven (325 degrees) for 45 minutes, or until silver knife inserted in center comes out clean. This soufflé will not fall if it's left in a warm oven with the door open for a short time. Serves 6.

Easy Cheese Pudding

10 slices of bread
1/2 pound extra-sharp
  Cheddar cheese
2 cups milk
2 teaspoons Dijon mustard
3 eggs
Butter

Remove the crusts from the 10 slices of good quality bread, butter well and cut into cubes. Put in baking dish, alternating with grated cheese, then mix the following: milk, eggs (beaten), mustard.

Let stand several hours before baking in 275-degree oven for about 45 minutes. Serves 6 for luncheon. Garnish with sliced stuffed green olives or pitted black olives.

Finnan Haddie in Cheese Sauce

2 pounds finnan haddie fillets
1 1/2 cups Cheddar cheese,
  cubed
4 thin slices of Swiss cheese
1 teaspoon Dijon mustard
2 tablespoons flour
3 tablespoons butter
2 cups milk
1 ounce sherry
Salt and freshly ground black
  pepper

Cut the fillets into 1-inch pieces and poach them for 10 minutes; drain and set aside.

Melt the butter in a skillet, remove from the heat, add flour, and stir well.

Add the milk a little at a time, stirring constantly. Return to the fire and add the cubed cheese, stirring until it melts and is smooth. Add the mustard and stir it in.

Add the poached haddock chunks and the sherry. Season to taste with salt and freshly ground black pepper.

Place the mixture in an ovenproof baking dish and cover with a layer of slices of Swiss cheese. Bake in a 350-degree oven until the cheese is melted and light brown. Serves 4.

Cheese, Rice, and Olives

1/2 cup cooked rice
1/2 pound sharp Cheddar
  cheese, cubed
1 cup milk
1 egg, beaten
1/4 teaspoon salt
Pepper
1 cup stuffed olives

Melt cheese in milk, add egg, salt, and pepper; fold in rice. Put a layer of rice mixture in buttered casserole, then a layer of sliced stuffed olives. Alternate the layers of rice and olives and cover with buttered crumbs. Bake in a moderate oven. Serves 4. A simple, delicious luncheon dish.

Stuffed Crabs au Gratin

2 pounds meat from boiled
  crabs
12 crab shells
3/4 cup grated Gruyere
  cheese
1/2 cup chopped fresh
  mushrooms
1/2 teaspoon powdered
  mustard
Pinch of nutmeg
1 cup milk
1 cup cream
2 tablespoons flour
3 tablespoons butter
Freshly ground black pepper

How to Make the Cheese Sauce:
Melt the butter in a skillet, remove from heat; add the flour and mix thoroughly. Then add the milk little by little, stirring constantly. Add the cream the same way.

Return to the fire and add the grated cheese, stirring to make a smooth mixture.

Add the mushrooms, mustard, nutmeg, salt, and freshly ground black pepper.

How to Fill the Crabshells:
Place a layer of this sauce in the bottom of each crab shell, then fill the shell with crabmeat. Cover the top with another layer of sauce. Bake in a moderate oven until lightly browned on top.

Cheese and Squash Pie

I made this wonderfully different pie for an outdoor cocktail buffet last summer, and everyone had good things to say about it.

For the Dough:
2 sticks (1 cup) unsalted
    butter chilled and cut into
    bits
1/2 teaspoon salt
3 large egg yolks
3 cups unbleached all-
    purpose flour

For the Filling:
1-pound butternut squash,
    halved and seeds and
    strings discarded
1-pound acorn squash, halved
    and seeds and strings
    discarded
3 large carrots, cut into
    1/4-inch pieces
1 large onion, chopped
The white part of 1 leek,
    halved lengthwise, washed
    well, and chopped
3 tablespoons unsalted butter
1 tablespoon dried tarragon,
    crumbled
3/4 cup whole-milk ricotta
1 large whole egg
1 cup freshly grated Romano
2 cups grated sharp Cheddar
3 large egg whites, beaten
    lightly

How to Make the Dough:
In a food processor, blend the butter with the salt and the egg yolks until the mixture is just combined, add the flour, and blend the mixture until it resembles meal. Transfer the mixture to a bowl and toss it with 3 to 5 tablespoons ice water, or enough to just form a dough.

Divide the dough into two balls, one slightly larger than the other. Dust the balls with flour and chill them, wrapped loosely in wax paper, for at least 1 hour and up to 12 hours.

How to Make the Filling:
Bake the squash, cut sides down, in a buttered jelly-roll pan in a preheated 350-degree oven for 45 minutes to 1 hour, or until it is tender. Let the squash cool and spoon the pulp into a bowl. In a saucepan bring 1 cup water to a boil, add the carrots, and boil them for 5 minutes or until they are tender. Drain the carrots and add them to the squash. In a skillet, cook the onion and the leek in the butter over moderately low heat, stirring until they are softened. Add the tarragon, cook the mixture, stirring, for 1 minute, and add it to the squash mixture, the ricotta, and the whole egg until the mixture is smooth, and in a bowl combine the mixture with the Romano, the Cheddar, and salt and pepper to taste.

Roll the larger ball of dough carefully in a 13-inch round on a well-floured surface, fit it gently into a 9-inch quiche pan with a 2-inch removable fluted rim, and patch

any tears. Fill the dough with the squash mixture and moisten the edge of the dough lightly with water. Roll the other ball of dough carefully into a 10-inch round on the well-floured surface and lay it carefully over the filling. Press the edges of the dough together gently, cut off the excess and crimp the edge decoratively. Brush the dough with some of the egg white and bake the pie in a preheated 425-degree oven for 50 minutes to 1 hour, or until the crust is golden. Let the pie cool on a rack, remove the rim of the pan carefully, and transfer the pie to a serving plate. Serves 6 to 8.

Crabmeat au Gratin en Casserole

1 pound crabmeat chunks
2 scallions and 3 inches of
　green, chopped
1/4 cup sauterne
1/8 cup sherry
1 cup cheese sauce (see
　recipe on page 41)
4 slices toasted bread
1/4 cup Parmesan cheese
Butter

Combine the first five ingredients. Cover the bottom of a casserole with toast slices and place the crab mixture on top of the toast. Sprinkle with Parmesan cheese. Bake in a 350-degree oven for 10 or 15 minutes or until the top is brown.

Ricotta and Black Olive Puree for Pasta

1/2 cup ricotta cheese
1/2 cup heavy cream
1/4 cup purée of black Italian
　or Greek olives
1/2 cup freshly grated
　Parmesan
2 tablespoons butter, at room
　temperature
1 tablespoon salt
2 tablespoons vegetable oil
1 pound pasta—choose
　Rigatoni or some other
　heavy tubular pasta. Cook
　al dente.
1/4 cup finely chopped fresh
　parsley
Freshly ground pepper

Blend the ricotta and heavy cream in a heavy saucepan over very low heat until smooth. Remove from the heat and stir in the olive purée and the Parmesan. Place the butter, cut into small pieces, in a large, warm bowl.

Place the cooked pasta in a large bowl and toss with the butter. Add the cheese/olive purée, toss again. Add the parsley and pepper. Remember to place the bowl of freshly grated Parmesan on the table, along with the pepper mill. Serves 8.

F I S H

What female heart can gold despise?
What cat's averse to fish?
—Thomas Gray, "Ode on the Death of a Favorite Cat"

Being brought up a Catholic makes it difficult to like fish. The church's restriction against eating meat on Fridays made the eating of fish almost mandatory, and nobody likes to do what they have to do. Also being brought up in Pittsburgh made it difficult to buy fresh fish on Fridays, or any other day for that matter. Local markets, like our regular A&P, didn't carry fresh fish during the days I did the shopping for our family.

When I entered high school I had to take four semesters of a domestic science course and, of course, I chose Food I, II, III, and IV. That's when I really learned about fish, about its nutritive values—the minerals and oils and fats it contains—and about its low calorie content. Miss Eckert, my senior foods teacher, felt that Midwesterners didn't understand or appreciate the culinary pleasures of seafood. She embarked on a one-woman crusade to lead her foods students out of ignorance and into a glorious awareness of the variety and delectable flavors of a wide array of fish dishes. We had to learn how to shop for fish at the big market downtown, how to tell fresh fish from not-so-fresh, how to poach, bake, broil, flake, and sieve fish for everything from cod fish balls to baked stuffed flounder. Shrimp was excluded—that was too expensive—but we did learn a great recipe for sautéed fillet of sole with paprika and butter sauce, and a number of quick ways to bake fillets that tasted good enough to get my younger sister and brother to eat them.

I'm grateful to Miss Eckert for introducing me to one of the culinary delights of life.

Fish in my kitchen creates a state of siege. Sidney smells it, sees it, wants it. There's no time to be lost as far as he's concerned. His only thought is to get as much as possible of the fish or the fillets or the shrimp before I manage to clean and cook them. Because fish supplies so many needed nutrients for cats, I'm quite willing to share, but at my speed and in the quantities I can spare. (Red meat tuna and oily fish are not good for cats, however, because of the oxidizing of vitamin E. And fish should always be cooked before cats eat it, although Sidney will take it any way he can get it.) Miss Blue doesn't try to prowl the counter and remove a fillet in toto; instead, she sits still and adds to the confusion by singing a loud paeon of pleas. Blue's fish song and Sidney's forays bring quick action from me. They each get a nice bit of that which they covet and then they are ostracized to the bathroom where their box is and where they have taken over one shelf in the linen closet for their naps. In the calm that follows, I take my time to prepare whatever delectable creature from salt- or fresh water that has been chosen for that night's dinner party.

The recipes included here are all tried-and-true favorites of Sidney's, Miss Blue's, and mine. Remember: Be certain the fish is fresh, the flesh firm, and the eyes bright, not cloudy. The fresher the fish, the better the dish. And don't overcook!

Baked Mackerel with Mushroom Sauce

2 whole mackerels
1/4 cup white wine
2 scallions and 2 inches of green leaves
6 mushrooms, chopped finely
1 small onion, chopped
1 tablespoon chopped parsley
1 clove garlic, finely minced
3/4 stick butter
3 tablespoons flour
1 cup light cream
1 cup evaporated milk
3 egg yolks, beaten

Place mackerels in a buttered baking pan. Sprinkle with white wine, 2 mushrooms finely chopped, and 1 scallion finely minced. Bake for 15 minutes in a preheated 350-degree oven. Place each fish on a warm serving dish and keep it hot while making the sauce.

How to Make the Sauce:

Add the pan juices to a skillet with 1/4 stick of butter; add the onion, minced scallion, garlic, parsley, and mushrooms and sauté until the vegetables are soft. Season with salt and freshly ground black pepper. Melt 1/2 stick of butter in another skillet and add the flour, stirring well to form a roux. Add the cream and evaporated milk and stir constantly until the sauce thickens. Beat the egg yolks in a cup and add 2 tablespoons of the hot cream sauce to them slowly. Add to the main portion of the cream sauce. Add the vegetable mix to the cream sauce. Pour the sauce over the mackerel and serve at once, piping hot. Serves 2.

Broiled Mackerel

A freshly caught mackerel is one of the tastiest of all fish. Its meat is sweet, light and delicate enough to please the palate of the most exacting connoisseur.

Brush cleaned mackerel with melted butter, place on a buttered sizzle platter or broiling pan skin side down, and broil for 8 or 10 minutes.

Garnish with parsley and lemon wedges and serve.

Mackerel with Anchovy and Rosemary

Place 4 mackerels on buttered sizzle platters; brush with melted butter. Cut anchovy fillets in 1/4-inch pieces and dot the fish with these pieces. Sprinkle with dried rosemary leaves. Broil on one side only for 10 minutes or until the flesh flakes easily. Garnish with parsley and lemon wedges, and serve piping hot. Serves 4.

Coquille St. Jacques

2 cups bay scallops or sea
   scallops, quartered
   (1 1/2 pounds)
2 cups dry white wine
2 lemon quarters
1 bay leaf
3/4 cup milk
3/4 cup cream
3/4 cup grated Swiss cheese
2 tablespoons flour
1/3 stick butter
Salt and freshly ground black
   pepper

Heat the wine with the lemon quarters, squeezed, and the bay leaf; add the scallops and poach them gently until they are firm and opaque white. Remove the scallops and set aside and keep warm.

Melt the butter in a saucepan, remove from the heat and add the flour and mix well; then add the milk and cream a little at a time, stirring constantly. Add 1/4 cup of the poaching wine and stir it in. Return to the fire and add the grated Swiss cheese (saving a little for topping), stirring until it melts and makes a smooth mixture. Add the scallops and season with salt and freshly ground black pepper to taste. Place the scallops and sauce on four large sea scallop shells. Sprinkle with Swiss cheese and brown lightly under the broiler flame. Serves 2 to 4.

Stuffed Crabs

2 pounds crabmeat
12 crab shells
1/2 cup chopped parsley
1 green pepper, finely
   chopped
1 clove garlic, minced
1 large onion, chopped
3 cups bread crumbs
1 stick of butter or more,
   melted
2 tablespoons sherry
Freshly ground black pepper
   to taste

Mix the vegetables with the bread crumbs, add melted butter, add crabmeat and salt and pepper to taste. Mix well and divide into 12 parts and fill the crab shells with the mix. Bake in a 350-degree oven until golden brown. Before serving, brush the tops with melted butter and sprinkle with a few drops of sherry. Serves 4.

Wellfleet Oysters Bienville

2 dozen Wellfleet oysters on
  the half shell
4 scallions and 2 inches of
  their leaves, chopped (or 1
  chopped onion)
3 tablespoons flour
2 tablespoons butter
1/2 cup chicken or fish broth
1 1/2 pounds shrimp,
  chopped
1 cup chopped fresh
  mushrooms
3 egg yolks
1/4 cup white wine
1/2 cup cream
Dash of Tabasco
Salt and pepper to taste

Place rock salt in pans and place oysters on top of the salt. Bake until about half done (7 minutes). Remove oysters and shells to baking/serving dish.

Prepare Bienville white wine sauce in advance as follows: Sauté the scallions in butter until golden, add the flour, browning it; add the broth. Add the mushrooms and the chopped shrimp.

Beat the egg yolks, the wine, and the cream together well; put them in the sauce, stirring rapidly to prevent curdling.

Add the Tabasco and salt and pepper to taste. Allow to cook for 10 to 15 minutes. Spoon the sauce over the oysters, covering each oyster well.

Sprinkle with mixed bread crumbs, paprika and cheese. Bake in the oven until light brown. Serves 4.

Salmon Dumplings

1 recipe biscuit dough
3/4 pound fresh salmon
  baked or poached
1/2 cup coarsely chopped
  sautéed mushrooms
2 tablespoons lemon juice
3 tablespoons minced fresh
  basil
1 recipe cheese sauce

Roll out biscuit dough to 1/4-inch thickness; cut into 4-inch squares. Mix salmon, mushrooms, lemon juice, and minced basil. Put a generous mound of salmon mixture on each square of dough, bring corners of dough up around filling and pinch closed.

Place on greased baking sheet and bake in hot oven for about 20 minutes. Serve with hot cheese sauce, laced with lemon juice to taste. This is a great recipe for leftover salmon. Serves 2.

Baked Haddock

1 six- to eight-pound haddock
2 onions, chopped
2 small green peppers, diced
2 cloves garlic, minced
1 cup fresh mushrooms,
    chopped
1 can plum tomatoes
1/2 teaspoon ground cumin
1/2 teaspoon saffron
1 cup white wine
4 tablespoons olive oil
Fresh chopped parsley
1 onion, sliced
1 tomato, chopped
Freshly ground black pepper

Heat the olive oil in a skillet and sauté the onion, green pepper, garlic, and mushrooms until the vegetables are transparent. Add the cumin and saffron and stir them in; add the tomatoes, up, and cook slowly for twenty minutes more. Rub the fish inside and out with salt and pepper and melted butter, and lay it in a greased baking pan. Sprinkle it with the wine then ladle the tomato sauce over it. Spread slices of fresh tomato and onion over it. Bake 30 to 40 minutes in a 350-degree oven, basting with the sauce. Serves 4 to 6.

Patient, persistent Miss Blue doesn't care that she's sitting on a clean table set for brunch.

Halibut Florentine

1 pound halibut fillets,
  poached or baked
1 package frozen chopped
  spinach or 2 pounds fresh,
  cooked and chopped
  spinach
1 cup sour cream
1 egg yolk, chopped
2 tablespoons grated onion
1/2 cup freshly grated
  Parmesan
2 tablespoons butter

Put cooked fillets in individual baking dishes. Melt butter in saucepan, add frozen spinach and onion. Stir onion into butter, then cover saucepan and cook over low heat until spinach is defrosted (about 5 minutes). Add egg yolk, sour cream and mix well. Cover each fillet with spinach mixture, sprinkle with Parmesan. Broil until bubbly and cheese is lightly browned. Serves 2.

Anchovy Sauce for Broiled Salmon or Mackerel

2 tablespoons anchovy paste
2 tablespoons lemon juice
1/4 pound butter
Dash of Tabasco sauce

Mix anchovy paste and lemon juice in skillet with melted butter. Add Tabasco to taste and pour over broiled fish fillets just before they are ready to serve. Return to broiler for two minutes. Makes enough sauce for two servings.

Poached Salmon and Cream Sauce for Pasta

4 cups water
4 cups dry white wine
1 onion, quartered
5 sprigs parsley
1 celery stalk, chopped
1 carrot, peeled and chopped
2 cloves garlic, smashed
5 peppercorns
2 egg yolks
1/2 cup heavy cream
1/4 cup finely chopped fresh
　　parsley
1/4 cup finely chopped fresh
　　basil or tarragon (dry herbs
　　won't work in this recipe)
2 tablespoons vegetable oil
1 pound angel hair pasta
1 sweet red pepper, seeded
　　and sliced into very thin
　　strips
2 pounds fresh salmon steaks
2 tablespoons white-wine
　　vinegar
2 tablespoons lemon juice
2 tablespoons dry white wine
1 cup olive oil
2 teaspoons Dijon mustard
Freshly ground pepper
Chopped parsley

How to Poach Salmon Steaks:
Combine the first eight ingredients in a skillet, bring to a boil, and simmer, partially covered, for 30 minutes.

Add the salmon steaks to the liquid, completely covering. If more liquid is needed, add 1/2 white wine and 1/2 water. Simmer, partially covered, until the fish flakes, about 7 minutes, remove from heat.

When the fish is cool enough to handle, remove to a plate and strain the liquid into a bowl, and reserve it. Remove the skin and bones from the salmon, break the fish into small pieces, and add the fish to the strained liquid. Reserve.

Mix white wine vinegar, lemon juice, white wine, olive oil, mustard with two well-beaten egg yolks. Whisk well, add heavy cream. Cook angel hair pasta al dente in four quarts boiling water mixed with 2 tablespoons vegetable oil. Add herbs and red pepper to sauce. Drain salmon, mix with cooled angel hair, add sauce. Serves 4.

Crabmeat Mousse

2 envelopes unflavored
  gelatin
2 tablespoons dry sherry
1 cup chicken broth, boiling
2 egg yolks
1 cup heavy cream
3 tablespoons lemon juice
5 drops Tabasco
2 cups crabmeat
2 small stalks celery, roughly
  cut
2 tablespoons scallions,
  finely chopped
4 sprigs parsley
1/4 teaspoon margarine
1/4 teaspoon thyme
1/2 cup mayonnaise
Lettuce for garnish

Place gelatin and sherry in blender or food processor and set aside for 2 minutes until softened. Add boiling chicken broth and blend at low speed 10 seconds or until gelatin is dissolved.

Continue blending at low speed and add egg yolks, cream, lemon juice, Tabasco, crabmeat, celery, scallions, parsley, margarine, and thyme. Blend until smooth and well mixed.

If size of container is sufficient for mayonnaise, add it and blend 10 more seconds. If container is not large enough, pour crabmeat mixture into mayonnaise, using wire whisk to blend.

Pour into lightly oiled 6-cup mold. Chill.

Unmold onto platter and garnish with assorted greens. Serves 6.

Crabmeat Slaw with Tomato Juice Dressing

2 cups finely shredded
  cabbage
1 chopped pimiento
1 onion, grated
1 small cucumber, peeled
  and diced
1 chopped green pepper
1/2 cup finely cut celery
1 can crabmeat

Mix all together and add:
3/4 cup tomato juice
1 teaspoon dry mustard
1 teaspoon Worcestershire
  sauce
1 tablespoon lime or lemon
  juice
1 tablespoon mayonnaise
1/4 cup vinegar
1 teaspoon sugar
1 teaspoon salt, or more to
  taste
1/8 teaspoon black pepper
Few drops Tabasco sauce

Serve slaw well chilled on chilled plates, garnished with greens and lemon wedges.

Sour Cream Dill Sauce

1 egg
1 teaspoon salt
Pinch of freshly ground black
  pepper
Pinch of sugar
4 teaspoons lemon juice
1 teaspoon grated onion
2 tablespoons finely cut fresh
  dill
1 1/2 cups sour cream

Beat the egg until fluffy and lemon-colored. Add the remaining ingredients, blending in the sour cream last. Stir until blended and chill.

Anchovy French Dressing

1 small can flat anchovy
  fillets, drained
1/2 cup olive oil
2 tablespoons chopped
  parsley
1 tablespoon lemon juice

Mash the anchovy fillets with a fork. Combine the olive oil, lemon juice and mix until thoroughly blended. Add parsley and refrigerate until ready to serve.

Tuna Fish, Anchovies, and Capers Sauce for Spaghetti

4 tablespoons olive oil
1 small onion, chopped fine
2 cloves garlic, minced
2 cups canned Italian
  tomatoes drained, seeded,
  and chopped
1/2 teaspoon basil
2 tablespoons capers
Salt and freshly ground
  pepper
2 tablespoons softened
  butter
10 anchovy fillets, finely
  chopped
1 six-and-a-half-ounce can
  tuna fish
2 tablespoons vegetable oil
1 pound spaghetti
1/4 cup chopped fresh parsley

In a saucepan, heat 3 tablespoons of the oil over moderately low heat and in it sauté the onion until soft. Add the garlic for the last minute of cooking. Add the tomatoes and simmer, covered, for 15 minutes. Add the basil, capers, 1/2 teaspoon of salt, and pepper to taste and simmer another 15 minutes.

While the tomatoes are cooking, mash the anchovies and butter together in a small bowl with a wooden spoon. Set aside. If the tuna is packed in olive oil, drain a tablespoon of the oil into a small skillet (discard the rest) and sauté the tuna over moderate heat for 2 or 3 minutes, breaking it into small pieces. If the tuna is not packed in olive oil, drain it completely and sauté in the remaining tablespoon olive oil. Set aside.

How to Cook the Spaghetti:
Boil 4 quarts of water, add vegetable oil, the spaghetti, stir, and cook until al dente. Drain, toss the spaghetti with tomato sauce, the anchovy butter, the tuna fish, and chopped fresh parsley. Serves 4.

Crabmeat Sauce for Linguine or Fusilli

My sister, Eleanor Davis, brought this recipe back from Italy. She said the original called for penne (pasta that is short and tubular and cut diagonally at both ends) but she prefers linguine (extra fine). I tried it with linguine and liked it but then I decided that fusilli, a spiraled spaghetti, would hold the sauce better. I recommend it.

1 six-ounce can of crabmeat
2 tablespoons butter
1/2 teaspoon hot pepper
   flakes or Tabasco to taste
1 cup fresh tomato sauce
   (see page 113)
1/2 cup brandy
1/2 cup cream
1 teaspoon paprika
2 tablespoons parsley,
   minced

Melt butter in large skillet, add pepper flakes and crabmeat (don't drain). Flame with brandy then add tomato sauce. Meanwhile, the water for the pasta should be on the stove and about ready to boil. Cook the pasta al dente and drain thoroughly, then put it into the sauce. Add cream and paprika, mix well and sprinkle parsley over it. Serve in warm bowl. Serves 4.

Seafood Lasagna

2 tablespoons butter
4 chopped shallots
3/4 pound shrimp
1 pound bay scallops
1/2 cup dry white wine
1 bay leaf
1 lemon, quartered
2 cups mushrooms, sliced
2 cups Bechamel sauce
1/2 cup heavy cream
1/4 teaspoon hot pepper
   flakes
3 tablespoons fresh parsley,
   chopped fine
8 flounder fillets, or scrod,
   poached lightly
1 pound fresh spinach
   lasagna
1 cup grated Swiss cheese

In a large skillet, melt the butter, add the shallots and sauté slowly. Then add raw shelled shrimp and bay scallops. Stir and cook over low heat for a few minutes until fish is cooked. Add white wine, mushrooms, Bechamel sauce, heavy cream, hot pepper flakes, and parsley and stir lightly until heated through. Now alternate layers of slightly cooked fresh spinach lasagna in buttered baking dish with fish and sauce mixture to fill the dish. Sprinkle cheese on top and bake to heat through. Place under the broiler for a few minutes to let the cheese brown lightly. Serves 8. (This is one of Sidney's favorite fish dishes.)

Anchovy and Black Olive Sauce for Pasta

4 cloves garlic, minced
3 tablespoons olive oil
10 anchovy fillets, chopped
3 cups canned Italian
tomatoes, not drained
1/2 pound black Italian olives,
pitted and sliced
2 teaspoons capers, drained
2 tablespoons chopped fresh
basil
1 teaspoon red pepper flakes
2 tablespoons vegetable oil
1 tablespoon salt
1 pound penne or other
tubular pasta

Sauté the garlic in the oil over moderately low heat; don't let it brown.

Add the anchovies and tomatoes and simmer for 5 minutes, stirring occasionally, to break up the tomatoes and prevent burning.

Stir in the olives, capers, basil, and red pepper flakes. Simmer, uncovered, for 45 minutes until the liquid has reduced and the sauce is thickened.

How to Cook the Pasta:
Put penne in 4 quarts of boiling water with vegetable oil added. Stir and cook until al dente. Drain; toss with sauce (reheat if necessary). Serve with a bowl of freshly grated Parmesan. Serves 4 to 6.

Olives, Scallops, and Red Peppers with Fusilli

1 cup freshly squeezed lime
juice
2 cloves garlic, crushed and
chopped
Peel of 1/2 lemon
3/4 pound sea scallops,
quartered
Salt and freshly ground black
pepper
2 tablespoons vegetable oil
1 pound fusilli
1/4 cup olive oil
2 roasted red peppers, cut
into 1 by 1/2-inch pieces
2 tablespoons capers
1/2 pound black olives, pitted
and quartered
2 tablespoons chopped fresh
basil

Marinate the scallops in the lime juice, garlic, and lemon peel. Cover and refrigerate for at least 5 hours.

How to Cook the Fusilli:
Boil 4 quarts of water; add vegetable oil, the fusilli, stir, and cook until al dente. Be sure not to overcook. Drain. Toss with olive oil; combine the red peppers, capers, olives, salt and pepper to taste, and toss gently. Remove the scallops from their liquid, and add them to the serving bowl with the fusilli and basil. Toss again and serve immediately.

Bouillabaisse

1 pound haddock
1 pound flounder
1 pound mackerel
1 pound shrimp in their
 shells
2 dozen shucked oysters
2 dozen littleneck clams in
 their shells
2 dozen mussels in their
 shells
4 scallions and 2 inches of
 green leaves, chopped
1 cup olive oil
2 onions, chopped
7 cloves garlic, minced
1 thirty-two-ounce can plum
 tomatoes
1 bay leaf
1/2 cup chopped parsley
1 lemon, sliced
1 cup white wine
1/2 teaspoon saffron
Fish stock as needed
Salt and pepper

Sauté the onion and garlic in the olive oil until transparent, then put in a large pot or a large earthenware casserole. Add the tomatoes, parsley, bay leaf, lemon slices and saffron. Now add the fish, shrimp and oysters. On top of this lay the mussels and clams. Add the wine and enough fish stock to cover the whole by 2 inches. (You should prepare the stock in advance by boiling the heads, bones and trimmings of the fish along with chopped onions, celery, parsley, thyme, basil, bay leaves, salt and pepper for 30 to 45 minutes. Strain it.)

Cover the pot, bring to a brisk boil, and cook for 15 minutes; it may take a little longer if you're cooking a really big batch, but don't overcook it. Another tip is to adjust the salt properly; remember, the shellfish juices are salty too. Cover the bottoms of large bowls with thin slices of garlic bread and fill the bowls with the fish, shellfish and soup. Sprinkle parsley on the top.

Whole Stuffed Flounders

6 whole 1 1/2- to 2-pound
  flounders
1 cup chopped boiled
  shrimps
1 cup chopped scallops,
  lightly poached
1 large onion, chopped
4 cloves garlic, minced
1/2 sweet pepper, finely diced
1 stalk celery, minced
2 tablespoons chopped
  parsley
1 cup fresh mushrooms,
  chopped
1 teaspoon prepared mustard
1 tablespoon Worchester-
  shire sauce
Dash Tabasco
4 eggs
1/4 loaf French bread
1 tablespoon butter
1/2 cup sauterne
Salt and freshly ground black
  pepper

Keep the heads and tails on the cleaned flounders for appearance's sake. Lay the flounders flat and cut an "X" lengthwise on the body. Fold back the corners of the cut and lift out the backbone.

Sauté the celery, onion, garlic, green pepper, parsley and mushrooms until soft and golden. Add the shrimp and scallops. Moisten the bread until workable with the fingers; make a paste of it. Beat the Worcestershire sauce, Tabasco, sauterne and mustard into the eggs until thoroughly mixed. Pour this mixture over the bread, adding the sautéed vegetables, shrimp, and scallops; mix well.

Divide the mixture into 6 parts and stuff lightly into the cavities of the flounders. Sprinkle the fish with melted butter, salt and pepper and finely minced garlic.

Bake at 400 degrees until golden brown, about 25 minutes. Or broil them in butter about 4 inches from the flame, 6 or 8 minutes on each side. Place on hot serving plates and sprinkle with a tablespoon of sherry and chopped parsley. Serve at once, piping hot. Serves 6.

Old-Fashioned Scalloped Oysters

2/3 cup soft bread crumbs
1 cup fine cracker crumbs
1/2 cup butter, melted
1 1/2 pints small shucked
  oysters, or 18 large oysters
3/4 teaspoon salt
Freshly ground black pepper
  to taste
2 tablespoons chopped
  parsley
1/2 teaspoon Worcestershire
  sauce
3 tablespoons cream
1/2 cup sherry

Preheat oven to moderate (350 degrees).

Mix the bread crumbs, cracker crumbs and butter.

Place half the crumb mixture on the bottom of a greased one-quart casserole. Add half the oysters, reserving the liquor, and sprinkle with half the salt, pepper, and parsley. Add the remaining oysters and sprinkle with the remaining salt, pepper, and parsley.

Mix one-third cup oyster liquor with the Worcestershire sauce, cream and sherry and pour over the oysters. Top with the remaining crumb mixture. Bake, uncovered, until puffy and brown, about 45 minutes.

Salmon Mousse

1 envelope unflavored gelatin
1/4 cup cold water
1/2 cup boiling water
1/2 cup mayonnaise
1 tablespoon lemon juice
1 tablespoon grated onion
1/2 teaspoon Tabasco sauce
1/4 teaspoon paprika
1 teaspoon salt
2 cups canned salmon,
  drained and finely chopped
1 tablespoon chopped capers
1/2 cup heavy cream
3 cups cottage cheese

Soften the gelatin in the cold water, add the boiling water and stir until the gelatin has dissolved. Cool.

Add the mayonnaise, lemon juice, onion, Tabasco, paprika, and salt and mix well. Chill to the consistency of an unbeaten egg white.

Add the salmon and capers and beat well. Whip the cream, fold into the salmon mixture and turn into a two-quart oiled fish mold. Add the cheese to fill the mold. Chill until set.

Unmold on a serving platter and garnish with watercress, lemon slices and salmon roe. Serve with sour cream dill sauce (see page 54). Serves 8.

Broiled Salmon Steaks

Place the steaks of your choice on individual buttered sizzle platters or in a broiler pan. Brush with butter and lemon juice, sprinkle with salt and pepper. Place it 4 inches below the flame and broil for 5 minutes on each side, basting frequently with butter and lemon juice.

Serve with a broiled, stuffed tomato between the "wings" of each steak.

Baked Sole with Shrimp

2 pounds fillets of sole
24 small cooked shrimp
1 cup sour cream
1 cup chili sauce
1 cup white wine

Place fillets in individual buttered baking dishes. Arrange shrimp, about 6 to each serving, over fish. Mix sour cream, chili sauce and white wine. Pour over fish and lay 3 thin slices of lemon on each fillet. Bake for about 30 minutes. Serve with a tossed green salad and hot bread. Serves 4.

Baked White Fish Fillets with Sour Cream

1 pound fillets of halibut, sole, or other white fish, well seasoned
1/2 cup scallions, slivered
1/2 cup thin strips of fresh red pepper
4 tablespoons butter
1 1/2 cups sour cream

Sauté scallions lightly in melted butter. Add red pepper strips. Place fillets in same pan, cover with scallions and peppers. Bake in moderate oven for about 8 minutes; cover with sour cream, return to oven for about 10 minutes, until sour cream is lightly browned.

New England Clambake

How to Do a Kitchen-size Clambake:

It seems inappropriate to write a selection of recipes for fish without doing something on that delectable New England creation, the clambake. While researching the subject, I found a wide variety of ways to cook and present a clambake meal. One recipe is for 150 people and advocates the use of a new galvanized steel 30-gallon garbage can as the cooking utensil of choice. The author of that recipe warns that one must wash such a utensil with the contents of a box of baking soda mixed with warm water to neutralize any residue of the galvanizing process. I have not chosen to recommend that clambake recipe. One reason is that urban cat lovers would not have the facilities to cook anything in a 30-gallon utensil. I thought it best to combine the cooking technique of a kitchen clambake recipe with the ingredients (but not the quantity) suggested for a Provincetown clambake for 150 hungry beachcombers. Here it is:

125 littleneck clams
4 pounds haddock fillets
4 pounds linquica (Portugese sausages) if available, or Kielbasa (Polish sausage). I like the flavor of Kielbasa and can always find them in my local supermarket or butcher's shop
3 pounds best quality pork sausage links
24 new potatoes of medium size
24 small onions or 12 large onions cut in half
12 ears of corn
1/2 gallon dry white wine
1/2 gallon water

Wash the clams, discarding any whose shells are cracked or open. Handle carefully because littlenecks' shells are brittle and crack easily. Set aside.

Cut haddock into 4-ounce pieces. Cut the sausages into 3-inch pieces. Peel the onions. Wash and peel potatoes. Shuck the corn.

Now you are ready to make neat foil packages of all the ingredients except the clams. Use heavy-duty extra-wide aluminum foil and tear off pieces about 12-inches long. On the open sheet of foil lay an ear of corn, the sausages, two onions, two potatoes, then a piece of haddock. Wrap the bundles tightly and press them as flat as possible. Punch eight holes in each side of the bundle so cooking juices will circulate. Stack 12 bundles in bottom of 15-gallon cooking pot or clam steamer. Add 1/2 gallon wine and 1/2 gallon water to pot. Cover tightly. Put brick on top of lid to hold lid down tightly, if necessary. Place on stove, steam for about one hour.

Then open and place the clams on top of the packets. Steam for one half hour or more until clams are open. The clam juice will have seeped down into the packets and given the contents a delicious flavor. The broth in the bottom of the pot is usually extraordinarily good.

Serve clam broth first, then the clams with generous amounts of melted butter for dunking.

The sausages and vegetables are served last, always with a cold beer. This is a way to have a seashore classic on a city-size terrace or country house patio. If your cats are like mine, they will frequent the scene of this feast, hoping for a bit of clam or butter or haddock. And like mine, I hope they won't be disappointed.

E G G S

It's very *provoking to be called an egg,* — very.
—Humpty Dumpty

The egg, beautifully shaped and much prized as food since early civilizations, has had its good reputation somewhat tarnished in the last few years. The reason is that so much of the egg yolk is saturated fat—a forbidden food if one is battling cholesterol. The current wisdom is to eat only one egg yolk for every two called for in a dish, served with fat-free protein (see *Jane Brody's Good Food Book*). Since eggs are such inexpensive sources of protein, most nutritionists don't advocate the elimination of them from human or cat diets; they just suggest we take care and avoid fatty foods like organ meats if we're planning to enjoy eggs at a meal.

I for one am glad. Eggs do such wonderful things. In the right proportion they cause a runny mixture of flour and milk and melted butter to change into a large, golden-brown puff of a pancake after ten or so minutes in a hot oven. And egg whites beaten to snowy peaks with flour and sugar can turn into light, heavenly angel cakes. Eggs make miracles in cooking, which is part of the fun, and their versatility—the multitudinous ways they can be cooked—add to the pleasure of *cuisine a l'oeuf.*

I had always heard that a beaten raw egg shared between my two cats would do wonders for their coats. Apparently, that's true for dogs, but not for cats. As with meat, fish, and fowl, one should always cook eggs before feeding to cats. However, eggs *are* good for them because cats need more protein than dogs, and more fat. That explains why Miss Blue nudges the eggs I put out for my omelet with an insistent air—she knows they're recommended for her and she wants her share. Now.

Sidney is less interested in eggs unless I whip up an egg and fish mixture with a little bran and wheat germ, as recommended by cat nutritionists. Then he'll move his long black body in the direction of his dish and purr gratefully as I serve him. But Sidney's appetite appears to me, after almost nine years, to be really insatiable, while Miss blue recognizes her ladylike limits. Since she is full-blooded Siamese and he, I think, has some royal blood, I'm not surprised they both insist on an interesting and varied diet. Active breeds, such as Siamese, require more food than their more sedate cousins, the Persians. So I'd better hurry on with listing the egg recipes we like because the next chapter is on liver and kidneys, which really cause a *catastrophe* in my household.

Baked Eggs in Mashed Potato Nests

5 eggs
2 cups mashed potatoes
4 slices bacon, cooked until
  crisp
Salt to taste
Freshly ground black pepper

Crumble crisp bacon into mashed potatoes, stir in one egg and salt and pepper.

Put 1/2 cup mounds of potato mixture on buttered cookie tray. Indent top with a spoon and break an egg in the hollow. Bake in a moderate oven until the eggs are set, about 15 minutes.

Fried Eggs

Everyone may know how to fry an egg; but if you don't, here's how I do it.

1 1/2 tablespoon butter or bacon fat for each egg. Have the eggs at room temperature.

Melt enough butter or bacon fat in a heavy skillet to cover the bottom. Break the desired number of eggs into a saucer and slip them carefully in the pan.

Cook over low heat, basting the eggs with hot fat until the whites are almost set.

Add a tablespoon of water for each egg you are cooking; cover skillet for one minute. Baste whites with water until coated. Remove eggs with pancake turner. The whites are cooked but tender and the yolks are runny. Don't use this method if you like eggs cooked on both sides.

Oeufs au Buerre Noir

The most famous fried-egg dish is the French specialty, fried eggs *au buerre noir* or in black butter. Fry eggs in butter and transfer to a warm serving dish. Add a little additional butter to the pan and cook quickly until dark brown. Add a few drops of vinegar for each egg. Pour mixture over the eggs; garnish each with one-half teaspoon capers.

Spinach Soufflé

1 tablespoon butter
1 tablespoon chopped
   scallions
2 tablespoons grated cheese
1 1/2 tablespoons flour
1 cup milk
4 egg yolks
4 egg whites, beaten
3/4 teaspoon salt
Pepper
2 cups cooked, chopped
   spinach

Sauté scallions in butter. Stir in flour, add milk slowly. Add spinach, cheese, seasonings. Heat, remove from fire. Mix in unbeaten yolks. Cool, fold in whites. Pour into greased baking dish and set dish in pan of water in a moderate oven. Bake until mixture rises and sets, about 30 minutes. Serves 6.

Spinach Soufflé with Poached Eggs

8 eggs
1 ten-ounce bag spinach or
    about 1 pound fresh
    spinach
2 tablespoons butter
2 tablespoons flour
2 tablespoons grated
    Parmesan cheese
1/2 cup milk
Salt
Freshly ground black pepper
Nutmeg

Preheat oven to 425 degrees. Butter a six-cup soufflé dish.

Poach four eggs—one or two at a time—just long enough so that you can lift them from the simmering water with a slotted spoon, about two to three minutes. Drain and transfer the eggs to two or more saucers to cool.

Trim off large stalks and wash the spinach. Shake off as much water as possible. Blanch spinach over medium-high heat in an uncovered saucepan, stirring frequently. Do not overcook. Chop finely. Measure out 3/4 cup and squeeze out remaining moisture.

Melt two tablespoons of butter in a saucepan. Add the flour and one tablespoon of the cheese. Cook briefly. Add the milk and stir until smooth and thickened. Add the chopped spinach to this sauce.

Separate the remaining four eggs. Stir the yolks into the hot but not boiling sauce. Season with salt, pepper and nutmeg to taste. Transfer sauce to a good-sized bowl.

Beat egg whites with a pinch of salt until very stiff. Fold a small amount of the egg whites into the sauce to lighten it. Gently fold in the remaining egg whites.

Cover the bottom of the soufflé dish with several spoonfuls of soufflé mixture. Cook for four minutes in preheated oven.

Gently transfer the drained poached eggs onto the partially cooked layer of soufflé. Make a mark on the outside or bottom of the dish to indicate the location of the eggs. Spoon the rest of the soufflé mixture onto the eggs. Sprinkle the remaining cheese over top.

Bake the soufflé 12 to 15 minutes. The soufflé will have a good crust and will be slightly runny in the center. The poached eggs should be cooked, with the yolks still runny. Serves 4.

Little Girl Blue knows how to look pretty on the reflective surface of the dining room table.

Banana Soufflé

4 ripe bananas
2 well-beaten yolks
2 tablespoons melted butter
1/2 cup sweet or sour cream
1 tablespoon lemon juice
Grated rind of 1/2 lemon
1/4 cup sugar
2 egg whites
Pinch of salt
Cinnamon for dusting on
    soufflé

How to Make Meringue:
2 egg whites
6 tablespoons brown sugar
Pinch of salt

Purée bananas in food processor.
    Add the well-beaten yolks, butter, cream, lemon juice, and grated lemon rind.
    Fold in 1/4 cup sugar and, last of all, the whites, well beaten with the salt.
    Pour into 6 individual ramekins or baking cups, greased with butter. Dust with cinnamon. Set in a pan 1/4 full water and put in a moderate oven, 375 degrees.
    After the soufflé has been baking 15 minutes remove from the stove and top with meringue made by beating the 2 egg whites with a few grains of salt and 6 tablespoons of brown sugar.
    Cook 10 to 15 minutes longer, or until meringue browns slightly. Serve warm or cold. Serves 6.

Chicken Soufflé

How to Make the Mushroom Sauce:
6 tablespoons butter
6 tablespoons flour
2 cups milk
Salt and pepper to taste
1/2 cup fresh, chopped mushrooms
1 1/2 cups diced white meat of chicken

Melt the butter in heavy saucepan, stir in flour to make roux, add 2 cups milk, stirring constantly. Season, then add mushrooms to hot sauce. Remove from heat, add chicken. Cool.

How to Make Cream Sauce:
3 tablespoons butter
3 tablespoons flour
1 cup milk
Salt and pepper to taste
4 egg yolks (beaten)
4 egg whites (beaten)

Make the second sauce of the butter, flour, milk, salt and pepper according to directions above. Pour slowly on beaten yolks. Fold in stiffly beaten egg whites. Put mushroom mixture in bottom of buttered baking dish, then pour cream mixture on top. Set baking dish in pan of hot water. Bake in 325-degree oven for 40 minutes. Serves 4.

Puffy Oven Pancake

For two people:
2 well beaten eggs
2 tablespoons flour
2 tablespoons milk
2 tablespoons melted butter
Pinch of freshly grated
   nutmeg
Pinch of sugar (if you like)

Mix eggs, flour, and milk together in a bowl of appropriate size for the amount of batter you are making. Meanwhile, melt the butter in the baking dish that you will use to bake the pancake. You can double, triple, or quadruple this recipe. Just be sure the mixture covers the bottom of the baking dish you are using and that the dish is about 2 to 2 1/2 inches deep. Place the batter in with the melted butter—don't stir—then put in a heated 375-degree oven. Don't open oven while pancake is cooking or it will not rise properly. It takes about 8 minutes for the 2-egg version to rise; 10 or 12 for the 4-egg version, and so on. If you do open the oven before the mixture has puffed up, close it *immediately!* In another few minutes the pancake will be puffed up and lightly browned, and ready to pile high with crisp bacon, thin sautéed slices of boiled or baked ham or thin slices of Kielbasa, pan-browned in a little butter. Apple slices sautéed in butter, lightly sugared, with a little nutmeg and cinnamon added come next. (Any summer berry can be substituted; just heat them with 1/2 cup of sugar to 1 cup fruit. Cook until sugar is thoroughly dissolved.) Top meat and fruit mixture with sour cream and serve immediately.

Sidney checks out the oven pancake

K I D N E Y   A N D   L I V E R

Leopold Bloom ate with relish the inner organs of beasts and fowls.
He liked thick giblet soup, nutty gizzards, a stuffed roast heart, liver
slices fried with breadcrumbs, fried hencod's roe. Most of all he liked
grilled mutton kidneys ...
—James Joyce, *Ulysses*

... Ella Mason
For no good reason
Plays hostess to Tabby, Tom and increase
With cream and chicken-gut feasting and palates
Of finical cats.
—Sylvia Plath, "Ella Mason and Her Eleven Cats"

In the matter of enjoying liver and kidneys my father and Leopold Bloom are much alike. In fact, there are many similarities between Mr. Bloom and Mr. Morin, but such Joycean concerns take us too far away from recipes for calves liver sautéed with mustard sauce and Grandmother Morin's kidney stew. As far as feeding "finical cats" is concerned, nothing causes more of a ruckus between my cats than liver or kidney dishes.

My Grandmother Morin's kidney stew was often served in our home, and was regarded by my playmates as "horrid!" They'd add, "Tastes awful!" and "We never have *that!*" Such reactions added to my slowly growing belief that our family *was* strange—different from the Kelleys, the Pascasios, and the Wrights who all seemed more firmly centered and, well, *normal* than we did. Our meals at home were different from those at my friends' houses, more nicely served and better tasting, so I didn't mind our "irregular" status too much. While my young Pittsburgh friends were never invited to share kidney stew at our house, I very much enjoyed the rich gravy and thin slices of kidney pooled in mounds of mashed potatoes. The gravy was too good to be wasted, so when the potatoes were finished, we were allowed to have a slice of buttered bread in the center of the plate and another serving of that aromatic sauce.

For all the adult years of my life I have been grateful for that perceived "difference" of our family. It taught me one thing that has been a great help in living my life: that if it really tastes good and feels right, stick with the sauce you like and the goal you've set. Maybe that's another reason I like cats so much. Certainly when Miss Blue or Sidney smell fresh calves liver as I open the butcher's paper, they set an immediate goal: to have a bite of that liver as soon as possible, preferably before it's cooked, or even washed. Sidney leaps to the sinkside counter and Miss Blue starts a medley of her most persuasive songs. I have always capitulated to their demands and sliced them a nice piece of the beloved liver, cooked, then chopped into fine bite-size pieces to put in their saucers. This would detain them long enough for me to get on with the skinning and deveining of the meat.

I have referred to many cookbooks in the course of writing *The Cat Lover's Cookbook* just to be sure my directions are clear and easy to follow. In the matter of cooking kidneys I've discovered that many cookbooks don't include details about the trimming and skinning necessary in preparing kidneys. Therefore, you'll find more explicit directions below. Proper trimming is good news for the cats, too, since they can enjoy some of the trimmed portions, and can thus have a greater share of the feast!

How to Trim Kidneys:

Split the kidneys and remove the cores. Snip the white membrane with curved scissors. Large beef kidneys should then be soaked for two hours in cold, salted water. After soaking and drying, sauté the kidneys briefly over brisk heat and put aside to cool before further cooking. For easier slicing, place kidneys in a covered dish in the refrigerator. When cold, cut into thin slices or as specified in recipe. You are then ready to proceed with the stewing, broiling, or sautéing.

Quick and Easy Paté

Put the best quality 1/2 pound of liverwurst and a 3-ounce package of cream cheese to stand at room temperature until softened. Cream them together thoroughly until smooth. Add 1 tablespoon of Worcestershire sauce, 1/8 teaspoon of dry mustard, a dash of Tabasco; and a splash of brandy does wonders!

Chill. Serve in crock and garnish with black olives. Serve with thin slices of party rye bread or melba toast.

Quick Chicken-Liver Paté

1/2 pound chicken livers
Chicken broth to cover
2 hard-cooked eggs
1/2 cup chopped onion
2 tablespoons chicken fat or
    butter
Salt and freshly ground black
    pepper

Simmer the livers in broth until done, eight to ten minutes. Drain. Mix them with the eggs, using the steel blade of a food processor and a little of the liquid in which the livers were cooked.

Brown the onion lightly in the fat and blend all the ingredients to make a paste. Season with salt and pepper to taste. If desired, season further with a pinch of curry powder or a dash of cognac. Serve on buttered toast triangles.

"If I give you a bite of liver will you please get off the table?"

Chicken Liver Terrine

1 quart boiling salted water
1 stalk celery
2 sprigs parsley
6 whole peppercorns
1 pound chicken livers
1 1/2 teaspoons salt
Pinch of cayenne pepper, or
  1/2 teaspoon Tabasco sauce
1 cup soft butter
1/2 teaspoon nutmeg
2 teaspoons dry mustard
1/4 teaspoon powdered
  cloves
5 tablespoons minced onion
1/2 clove garlic, finely
  chopped
2 tablespoons cognac

To the boiling water add the celery, parsley and peppercorns. Reduce the heat and simmer five minutes. Add the chicken livers, cover and cook 10 minutes. Drain, chop the livers in the food processor.

Add the salt, cayenne, butter, nutmeg, mustard, cloves, onion, garlic, and cognac. Blend thoroughly. Pack in a three-cup terrine and chill thoroughly. Serve with buttered toast triangles. Makes about 3 cups.

Liver Dumplings

1/4 pound liver
  (veal or chicken)
1/2 small onion
1 egg yolk
1/4 teaspoon salt
Pinch of freshly ground black
  pepper
Pinch of nutmeg and of thyme
1 1/2 tablespoons minced
  parsley
1 1/2 slices bread without
  crusts
Milk or water
1/2 cup sifted flour,
  approximately
2 quarts soup stock

Trim the liver and grind with the onion, using the finest blade of the food processor. Add the yolk, salt, pepper, thyme, nutmeg and parsley.

Soak the bread in milk or water to moisten and squeeze out excess liquid. Add to the liver. Add enough flour to make a soft dough.

Bring the soup stock to a boil. Dip a teaspoon in the soup, then fill it with liver batter and drop the batter into the soup. Re-dip spoon in broth before shaping each dumpling. Cover the pot and simmer 10 to 15 minutes, depending on the size of the dumplings. Makes 3 to 4 dozen dumplings.

Mushrooms Stuffed with Liver

1 pound large mushrooms
5 tablespoons butter
1/2 pound chicken livers
1 tablespoon minced onion
1 three-ounce package cream
   cheese, softened
1/4 teaspoon powdered
   tarragon
Salt
Freshly ground black pepper
   to taste

Remove and chop the mushroom stems. In a skillet heat three tablespoons of the butter, add the mushroom caps and sauté 5 minutes, turning frequently. Remove to a platter.

Add the remaining butter to the pan and cook the chicken livers, mushroom stems and onion until the livers are lightly browned. Chop the liver mixture very fine in the food processor. Cool.

Cream the cheese, add the liver mixture and season with the tarragon, salt and pepper. Stuff the mushroom caps with the liver mixture. Makes 12 hors d'oeuvres.

Sautéed Calves Liver with Mustard Sauce

6 slices calves liver, trimmed
Salt and freshly ground black
   pepper to taste
About 3/4 cup flour
4 tablespoons butter

Dredge liver with flour seasoned with salt and pepper.

Sauté liver in melted butter over medium heat until golden brown on each side. Reduce heat and cook for 3 minutes to have liver just pink (the best way in my opinion). Put liver on heated platter and cover. Don't keep warm.

How to Make the Sauce:
2 tablespoons butter
2 tablespoons flour
1/2 cup Marsala
1 cup water
2 tablespoons Dijon mustard

Add butter to pan in which you sautéed liver. Scrape all the bits and pieces of browned flour into the butter and add a little water to loosen browned bits. Mix in flour until absorbed by butter. Add two tablespoons Dijon, 1/2 cup Marsala and stir together. Add 1/2 cup water, cook until thickened, adding remaining water if necessary. Taste for seasoning. Cover sautéed liver with sauce and put under broiler to warm quickly. Serves 4.

Sambal Goreng
(Chicken livers with vegetables from Indonesia)

1 pound chicken livers, cut in
  half
3 tablespoons peanut oil
10 cloves garlic, finely minced
1 teaspoon finely minced
  fresh ginger
3 shallots minced
1 pound string beans, in half-
  inch pieces
1/4 cup ground almonds
Juice of 2 lemons
1 tablespoon soy sauce,
  mixed with 1/2 tablespoon
  molasses
1 cup chicken stock
2 tablespoons salt
1 teaspoon hot red pepper
2 teaspoons brown sugar
2 teaspoons turmeric

In a large skillet sauté the chicken livers in peanut oil over high heat until lightly browned, stirring constantly. Remove the livers from the skillet.

Reduce the heat and add the garlic, ginger and shallots. Cook until the vegetables are soft, stirring occasionally. Add the string beans and cook three minutes.

Add the remaining ingredients, cover the pan and cook over low heat until the string beans are just tender, about ten minutes.

Return the livers to the pan and cook five minutes longer.

Serve with rice and imported soy sauce. Serves 6.

Chicken Livers Marsala with Italian Ham

1 pound chicken livers
1/4 cup butter
1/2 teaspoon salt
1/4 teaspoon freshly ground
  black pepper
1/2 teaspoon sage
2 slices prosciutto (Italian
  ham) diced
8 bread triangles, sautéed
1/4 cup Marsala
1 tablespoon butter

Cut the livers in half and simmer 5 minutes in melted butter with the seasonings and prosciutto.

Remove the livers from the pan and place them on the sautéed bread triangles. Add the wine to the pan gravy and cook three minutes. Add the remaining butter, mix well and pour over the livers.

Chicken Livers with Wine

1 pound chicken livers
4 tablespoons butter
4 tablespoons wine
  (sherry or Madeira)
2 tablespoons flour
Salt, pepper to taste
1/4 teaspoon sugar
1 pint chicken stock
1 clove garlic
3 sprigs parsley

Melt butter in skillet. Salt and pepper livers. Roll them in flour and sauté lightly in butter until golden-brown.

Add stock, garlic, and parsley and simmer 20 minutes or until livers are tender. Remove garlic and parsley from sauce and thicken with flour dissolved in water. Add sugar and wine.

Boil for an instant.

Serve over rice or an omelet.

Veal Kidneys Bordelaise

Salt and freshly ground black
  pepper to taste
6 veal kidneys, trimmed and
  cut into 1-inch slices
1/3 cup butter
1/4 cup chopped shallots
1/2 cup red Bordeaux wine
2 cups brown sauce
1 tablespoon chopped parsley

Salt and pepper the kidneys and brown them quickly in the butter in a skillet. Place in a chafing dish or casserole. Drain the fat from the pan.

Add the shallots and wine and boil until the wine is reduced one-third. Add the brown sauce and parsley and pour over the kidneys.

Heat just to simmering. Serve over toast, buttered noodles, or rice. Serves 8.

Veal Kidneys Flambé

1/4 cup butter
1 tablespoon chopped
  shallots
6 veal kidneys, trimmed and
  cut into 1-inch cubes
6 fresh mushrooms, sliced
2 tablespoons cognac
1/4 cup heavy cream
Salt and freshly ground black
  pepper to taste
Chopped parsley

Melt the butter in a skillet, add the shallots and sauté until tender but not browned. Add the kidneys and mushrooms and cook over moderate heat until lightly browned.

Warm the cognac and sprinkle over the kidney mixture. Ignite it and, when the flame dies, stir in the heavy cream. Cook one minute, or until the sauce thickens slightly. Season with salt and pepper and sprinkle with parsley. Serves 6.

English Beef and Kidney Pie

2 pounds beef chuck
1 pound beef kidney,
    carefully trimmed
2-inch piece of beef suet
1 large onion, coarsely
    chopped
1 cup rich beef stock
1 teaspoon salt
Freshly ground black pepper
Cayenne pepper
1 1/2 teaspoons Worcester-
    shire sauce
Flour
Pastry for a single-crust pie

Cut the beef and kidney into 1 1/2-inch cubes.

Fry the suet in a heavy kettle or Dutch oven. Remove suet cracklings. Add the onion and sauté until transparent.

Add the beef and kidney and cook, stirring almost constantly, until thoroughly browned.

Add the beef stock, salt, pepper and cayenne to taste and the Worchestershire sauce. Stir well, cover and simmer until the meat is tender, or about 1 hour and 45 minutes.

If necessary, add enough water to almost cover the meat. Thicken the broth with flour that has been blended with cold water (1 1/2 teaspoons of flour for each cup of broth). Transfer the mixture to a casserole and cool until lukewarm.

Preheat oven to hot (450 degrees).

Roll the pastry to 1/8-inch thickness and place over the meat, sealing it to the sides of the casserole. Cut gashes for the escape of steam. If desired, the pastry can be cut in strips and arranged lattice-fashion over the meat.

Bake about ten minutes, lower heat to moderate (350 degrees) and bake until the crust is delicately browned, or about fifteen minutes longer. Serve with English mustard.

Grandmother Morin's Kidney Stew

2 pounds young beef kidney
2 medium-to-large onions,
   sliced
3 tablespoons bacon fat
3 tablespoons flour
4 cups beef stock or bouillon
   made with cubes (last
   resort!)
Freshly ground black pepper
Fresh parsley, finely chopped
4 large Irish potatoes, peeled
   and cut into 2-inch pieces
(Note: you can serve the
   "stew" over mashed
   potatoes if you prefer)

Wash and trim the kidneys (see page 75). Cut into slices about 1/4-inch wide and 2-inches long.

Melt the bacon fat in a 4-quart Dutch oven over medium heat. Add the sliced onions, cook until almost brown. Take off heat. Put the pieces of kidney into a bowl, add the flour and coat them with it. You may need a little more flour, depending on how much trimming you had to do.

Now put the kettle back on the heat and when the bacon fat has heated thoroughly, add the kidney slices. Stir them around and slowly brown them in the fat and onion mixture. When all the kidney pieces are browned, add the stock and stir thoroughly. Cover, cook very slowly, stirring occasionally so the kidneys don't stick to the bottom of the pan. When kidneys are tender (taste to be sure), gravy should be thickened. If you are adding potatoes, do so now. Remove kidneys first and keep warm. If you like thicker gravy, the potatoes will help. If you want the gravy even thicker after potatoes have cooked, remove onions, and potatoes and add 1 or 2 tablespoons of flour (depending on how thick you like it) into 1/2 cup cold water. Blend until smooth, then slowly add to the hot sauce. Bring sauce to a boil, cook for at least 10 more minutes. Return kidneys, onions (they will have almost cooked away by now), and potatoes to the gravy. Add finely chopped fresh parsley and heat through.

Season to taste; serve with hot, crusty bread or rolls, sweet butter and a lightly dressed multi-greens salad. And think of James Joyce!

Sidney and Miss Blue, momentarily banished from the kitchen.

A P P E T I Z E R S

Before a cat will condescend
To treat you as a trusted friend
Some little token of esteem
Is needed, like a dish of cream;
And you might now and then supply
Some caviare, or Strassburg Pie,
Some potted grouse, or salmon paste—
He's sure to have his personal taste.
                    —T. S. Eliot, *Old Possum's Book of Practical Cats*

The succulent foods that T. S. Eliot suggested a person might give a cat to earn his esteem are all first-class appetizers. Several are listed by Craig Claiborne in his introduction to his fifty-page appetizer section in the first *New York Times Cookbook*. That book, a "good-luck-in-New-York" gift from a fellow copywriter in Pittsburgh, became my treasured standby cookbook for the large meals I prepared when my children were growing up. Christopher and Cass were always gratifying to cook for, and that encouraged me to try new recipes and different foods, some of which are famous failures. Ask them. I won't tell.

During the eleven years my late husband Michael and I had together, he always finished a meal by saying, "Thank you, Jane, that was good," or "delicious," or "exceptional," or some other term of approbation that made me glow and tell him how welcome he was.

As I mentioned earlier, I'm not a "do-it-by-the-book" cook. For a lot of years as a single parent, the budget didn't stretch to include much exotica, and I often found that recipes called for ingredients I couldn't find or afford. I learned from those years to take risks with substitute ingredients or cooking equipment.

When Mike and I were first renovating our loft in Soho I was taken with the desire to poach a salmon for a party appetizer, to serve whole with fresh dill and homemade mayonnaise. The eight-pound salmon cost a small fortune and when I measured it and my roasting pan I expected to use for the poaching process I saw the fish was much too large. I had planned to use my next-door neighbor's electric stove since our gas stove had not yet been hooked up (I had been cooking on a hot plate and electric skillets while we waited for the building to get approval for gas—not to come for three more years), but I refused to cut up the fish to fit into the roasting pan. And there was certainly no budget for a fish poacher after paying for the salmon. As I wondered what to do, I suddenly looked at my nice new dishwasher. Aha! Dishwashers spray lots of hot water for as long as twenty or thirty minutes. I could wrap the salmon in foil after seasoning it and giving it a splash of white wine, and lay it on the top rack of the dishwasher and put it through the wash and rinse cycle a couple of times until it had the equivalent of ten minutes per pound in hot water. I was very pleased with my idea because I was intent on serving whole, poached salmon, and nothing else would do.

Soon Hanne Tierney, my neighbor and a very good cook, stopped by to ask when I wanted to use her stove to poach the salmon. I pointed to the dishwasher and explained that the poaching was already in process. She gave me a funny look. By the time fellow co-opers came to the party that evening they had all heard how I cooked the salmon. They approached it with care, but in twenty minutes there was only skin where there had been eight pounds of pink and flaky salmon appetizer.

One of the original members of the co-op, Joel Dean, is one of the originators, along with Georgio DeLuca and Jack Ceglic, of that wondrous food and kitchen store, Dean & Deluca, on Prince Street in Soho. When I left the Wooster Street co-op last December to live in my little white house in the Hudson Valley, Joel said, "Remember the time you poached the salmon in the dishwasher?" That was fifteen years ago; I can't understand why he still remembers it. It seemed a perfectly sensible solution to me. And it still does.

Peppers or Pimientos and Anchovies

1 jar whole Italian peppers or
   Spanish pimientos
   (6 ounces)
2 cans flat anchovies
2 tablespoons lemon juice
3 tablespoons olive oil
2 lemons, cut into wedges
1/2 cup chopped fresh parsley
Romaine leaves, freshly
   washed and dried

Slice peppers in strips about 1/8 of an inch wide. Arrange pepper strips and anchovies criss-crossed on romaine leaves, in a serving dish. Mix lemon juice and olive oil in jar, shake well and season lightly. Remember the anchovies are salty and the pepper juice has a strong flavor. Pour mixture over anchovies and pimientos. Don't soak them, dribble it. Refrigerate to chill and marinate. Take out about one hour before serving so the flavors will not be dulled by the cold. Sprinkle all over with fresh parsley, finely chopped. Toast is good with this simple dish or Italian bread, with which to soak up excess dressing.

Olive Paté

12 ounces Mediterranean
   olives, seeded
1 stick sweet butter
1 clove garlic, crushed
4 cumin seeds, crushed

Put all ingredients in food processor; use steel blade and purée until smooth. Scrape every bit out of bowl into a pretty crock or dish; garnish with finely chopped pimientos, and chopped fresh parsley. Serve with thin slices of pumpernickle or rye bread.

Poor Cat's Caviar

1 jar red caviar (salmon roe)
1 cup sour cream
2 tablespoons lemon juice
   (approximately)
1 small package cream
   cheese, softened

Mix red caviar with softened cream cheese, add sour cream, lemon juice to taste. Mix gently so the caviar doesn't get squished. Chill, garnish with something green and serve with toast triangles, lightly buttered.

My cats will eat a little of the inexpensive caviar, particularly when fixed as above. The real stuff, which we have for great occasions, such as Cass and Jim's wedding, is what Sidney and Miss Blue especially like, and don't get much of. One thing to remember about fresh or pasteurized caviar: it must be chilled well before serving. That's why the great restaurants (and houses) always serve it in a bowl on a bed of ice. As long as we're on the subject, chopped hard-cooked egg whites, chopped hard-cooked egg yolks, and a bowl of finely chopped white onions or finely chopped scallions should accompany the caviar and buttered fresh toast. And lots of lemon wedges. To drink with it? Only chilled, high-quality vodka and the best dry champagne you can afford.

Red-Caviar Stuffing for Celery

2 bunches of celery
1/2 pound cream cheese
1 tablespoon grated onion
1/3 cup chopped parsley
1/3 cup red caviar
Salt and freshly ground black
   pepper to taste

Use choice, inner stalks of celery. Wash thoroughly.

Mix the softened cream cheese with the onion, parsley, caviar, salt and pepper. Stuff the celery stalks with the mixture and refrigerate until serving time. Serves 6.

Smoked Salmon

Buy the best salmon you can afford from Nova Scotia, Scotland, Norway, or Ireland. Slice very thin and serve on chilled plates with lemon wedges, capers, chopped white onions, or chopped scallions, buttered toast and the pepper mill. My cats love it without the accompaniments. It hurts to buy as much as you and your guests will want, but try.

Sardine Canapes

1 can boneless sardines,
  drained
2 tablespoons lemon juice
1 tablespoon cream
1/2 teaspoon dry mustard
1 tablespoon mayonnaise
Freshly ground black pepper
  to taste
Few drops of Tabasco sauce
Hard-cooked egg slices or
  sliced green olives

Mash the sardines with a fork and mix with the seasonings. Spread on toast rounds and garnish with hard-cooked egg slices or sliced green olives. Makes 12. Cats love these, so watch out!

Miss Blue makes her move while I'm busy with some last minute garnishing.

Cucumber Canapes

Neatly trim the crusts from fresh bread slices and cut each slice into four equal squares. Spread each square with softened butter. Peel cucumbers and cut into wafer-thin slices. Place a layer of cucumber slices on the bread squares.

Serve with salt, lemon wedges and freshly ground black pepper.

These are so good, inexpensive and easy-to-make. I include them because they are favorites of mine, rather than Sidney's or Miss Blue's. The cats only like the butter in this recipe.

Catapes

6 tablespoons of Roquefort
   cheese
1 tablespoon butter
1 teaspoon sour cream
3 slices white bread
6 tablespoons caviar
Lemon juice

Blend together the Roquefort cheese, butter and sour cream.

Toast the bread and spread with the cheese mixture. Top each slice with two tablespoons of caviar. Add a few drops of lemon juice. Cut each slice into four equal strips to get 12 canapes.

This recipe has a "punny" name because my cats love to eat all the caviar off the top, and did once when I ran to answer the doorbell and left a tray of the canapes, without lemon juice, exposed. So what better name for these? However, people like them very much, too.

Cooking under Blue's interested gaze from her perch on the KLH radio.

Stuffed French Bread

3 three-ounce packages of
   cream cheese
1 can anchovy fillets, rubbed
   to a paste
1 tablespoon capers or
   chopped sour pickle
2 tablespoons chili sauce
1 teaspoon grated onion
1 teaspoon Worcestershire
   sauce
3 dashes Tabasco sauce
Salt to taste
1/2 cup butter,
   at room temperature
1/2 cup minced watercress
1 tablespoon fine, soft
   bread crumbs
1 long loaf French bread

Cream the cheese until smooth in food processor. Add the anchovy paste, capers, chili, sauce, onion, Worcestershire, Tabasco and salt. Thin with liquid from the caper or anchovy container to spreading consistency.

Cream the butter, add the watercress crumbs; mix.

Split the bread lengthwise and remove the center. Spread the entire cavity of the upper half with watercress butter. Fill the cavity of the lower half with the cheese mixture, cover with top half of loaf. Wrap in foil, chill. Cut into thin slices before serving. Serves 12 to 14.

Anchovies with Onion Rings

6 anchovy fillets
1 clove garlic, minced
2 tablespoons parsley
1 teaspoon drained capers
2 tablespoons bread crumbs
1 cup olive oil
1/4 cup red wine vinegar
Salt and freshly ground
   black pepper
1 large white onion,
   sliced into rings

In a food processor, place the anchovies with one tablespoon oil from the can. Add the garlic, parsley, capers and crumbs.

Add the oil, vinegar, and salt and pepper to taste. Blend well and pour the mixture over the onions. Chill. Serve with chilled fish or meats. Serves 4 to 6.

Shrimp with Dill and Lime Sauce

1/2 cup sweet butter
2 pounds raw shrimp,
   shelled and deveined
Salt and freshly ground
   black pepper to taste
1 tablespoon chopped
   fresh dill
Juice of 2 limes
6 drops Tabasco sauce
1 teaspoon Worcestershire
   sauce

In a skillet heat the butter, add the shrimp and cook, shaking the skillet occasionally, until the shrimp are red in color and cooked through, about three minutes. Sprinkle with the remaining ingredients and serve on toothpicks. Serves 6.

Chilled Shrimp with Dill Sauce

1 quart water
1 tablespoon salt
1 stalk celery
1 carrot
Juice of 1/2 lemon
1/4 teaspoon cayenne pepper
1 small clove garlic
24 medium raw shrimp,
   shelled and deveined

In a deep saucepan, combine all the ingredients except the shrimp and boil 10 minutes.

Drop the shrimp into the boiling liquid and return to a boil. Cook 3 minutes and drain. Discard the vegetables and chill the shrimp. Serve with the dill sauce (see below).

How to Make the Dill Sauce:

3/4 cup olive oil
3 tablespoons lemon juice
Salt to taste
1/2 teaspoon dry mustard
1 tablespoon fresh
   chopped dill
1/2 clove garlic

Combine all of the above and mix well. Let stand overnight in the refrigerator. Discard the garlic and serve the sauce chilled. Serves 6.

Artichoke Bottoms with Shrimp

6 cooked artichoke bottoms
3 tablespoons olive oil
1 1/2 tablespoons wine
  vinegar
Salt and freshly ground black
  pepper to taste
1 cup cooked shrimp, cut
  into small pieces
1/2 green pepper, finely diced
1/3 cup mayonnaise
2 teaspoons lime juice
Paprika to taste
6 cooked whole shrimp

Cut off hard outer leaves of artichokes, the stem, and the top fourth of the leaves. Cook in water or chicken stock until tender; remove remaining leaves and with a sharp spoon remove the prickly chokes, leaving the smooth, tasty bottoms.

Marinate the artichoke bottoms in a mixture of the olive oil, wine vinegar, salt and pepper for about one hour.

Mix the cut-up shrimp, green pepper and mayonnaise seasoned with lime juice and paprika. Drain the artichoke bottoms and place on individual serving plates. Pile the shrimp mixture atop the artichoke bottoms, cover with a thin layer of mayonnaise and garnish each with a whole shrimp. Serves 4.

Hungarian Cheese

1 cup cottage cheese
1 cup butter
1 tablespoon caraway seeds,
  crushed or whole
1 tablespoon capers, minced
1 tablespoon chives, minced
1 tablespoon dry mustard
1 anchovy, chopped
1 tablespoon paprika

Put the cheese in a food processor. Add the butter with the caraway seeds, capers, chives, mustard and anchovy and process until blended together but not puréed. Chill. Serve mounded on greens or read on and do as I do.

I started to make this cheese for our annual holiday party because it is attractive, unusual, good-tasting, and within my budget. I make it appropriate for Christmas by spooning it on foil, wrapping it tightly, then shaping it into a roll. After chilling it to firmness, I unwrap it and roll it in Hungarian paprika and garnish it with some greens. I usually make about 6 rolls—about one recipe to a roll—and do the paprika bit before the holiday party begins so when one roll is eaten, there's another ready to put out. Served with thin slices of pumpernickle or Swedish rye, this is always a popular part of a buffet. I knew, from Craig Claiborne's *New York Times Cookbook*, that this recipe was a version of a Hungarian classic called Liptauer Kase. But when my Hungarian uncle, Laci, first tasted it at my house he was amazed. "Where did you ever learn to make Liptauer Kase?" he asked me. "It is our favorite in Budapest!"

He hadn't realized how international one can get without traveling the world when one reads great cookbooks.

"Now may I have my share?"

D E S S E R T S

Never eat more than you can lift.
                                            —Miss Piggy

Cooking is like love. It should be entered into with abandon or not at all.
                                            —Harriet Van Horn

To this day, at age eighty-nine, my father does not feel he has dined if he does not have dessert. Fortunately, his wife, Pauline, is a wonderful, inventive, creative cook who makes certain his good lunch or dinner is followed by a delicious, sometimes even exotic dessert. He's very fortunate and knows it, always commenting when my sister or daughter and I visit their Ohio home, "The cuisine at this address is excellent. And Pauline never forgets dessert!" Well, because of my father I can't forget desserts either. I learned from him how good they are because when he and my mother were together the same rule applied: "It's not a meal without dessert." I enjoyed the results: creamy rice puddings, layer cakes, sponge pudding with lemon sauce, fresh strawberry shortcake, pineapple upside-down cake and lemon meringue pie. There was always something sweet and good at the end of those family meals.

Today we're all much more weight-conscious (some of us have to be, but I'll not mention names) and so dessert is not served at most meals when only family is present. That doesn't mean we don't think about it, though, and when there are guests it's "just desserts" time.

My cats are glad when desserts are served and do their usual hanging around the counter number, on the lookout for cream or butter. Sidney likes white grapes very much, partly because they're fun to swat around, but he also bites into them and chews up a few.

My publisher knows of a cat who likes melon, particularly in the form of little balls. Cats are certainly experts in having fun, and even in the wild are known to play with their food before consuming it. Movable desserts, such as grapes and melon balls, provide hours of entertainment. Unfortunately, what's not eaten is left for someone to find and clean up. Squashed grapes on the living-room carpet may not seem like much fun to you.

Grapes and melon are good choices for dessert-loving cats because cats don't require carbohydrates in their diets and these fruits have very few.

I don't encourage Sidney or Miss Blue to partake of many of the sweets that go into the desserts I make, but the other day, while I was preparing a lemon mousse for a party, Sid "catjoled" me into giving him a taste. He ate every bit of the dollop I gave him and then looked at me yearningly, with those big, yellow-as-the-mousse eyes until I relented and gave him another taste. You have to have a very strong character to maintain your reserve with a cat like Sidney.

With caloric restrictions (the cats' and my own) in mind, I have not chosen recipes for chocolate mousse cake with brandied chocolate icing or browned butter and bourbon pie for listing below. Instead, you'll find quick and easy fruit puddings, some light soufflés and six mousses made with fruits, sugar, flavoring, and some whipped cream—easier than pie and much more appropriate for today's diets.

It's not fair to give you this statistic before you read the dessert recipes but an estimated 30 to 40 percent of American pets are overweight. It's about the same for their owners, so eat well, enjoy, but watch the pounds!

One of my standby dessert recipes for years has been raspberry mousse. It is made with 1 package of frozen raspberries (the only frozen berry besides blueberries I will use) mixed with 1/2 cup of sugar and 1/2 tablespoon lemon juice. Then the raspberry mixture is folded into whipped cream and put into a one-quart mold to freeze for two hours. It tastes lovely—not too sweet—and the color of the raspberries is beautiful with white cream.

I make hot raspberry sauce for the mousse with one package of frozen raspberries brought to boil, then reduced by one-third. Add some kirsch to flavor and serve hot over the mousse.

I always knew one could adapt the basic idea for this mousse recipe for use with other fruits so finally I took the time to try out some other fruits to include in this collection of sweet things!

Mandarin Orange and Kiwi Mousse

2 eight-ounce cans Mandarin
  oranges
2 kiwi fruits, peeled and
  sliced 1/4-inch thin
1 envelope of gelatin
2 ounces curaçao
1 cup heavy cream

Even though some New York City food writers say "Kiwi is out," this is a pretty and delicious combination.

Drain oranges, reserving juice, and set aside. Soften gelatin in 1/4 cup juice. Add curaçao. After gelatin has softened, heat mixture until gelatin dissolves; add drained oranges and kiwi slices to warm gelatin mixture. Cool. Whip 1 cup heavy cream to stiff peaks and fold into fruit and gelatin mixture. Put into clear glass serving dishes so the lovely colors of the fruit swirled with cream will show through.

You can top this with Chantilly cream if you're feeling particularly sybaritic. Just whip another 1/2 cup of heavy cream, mix in fine granulated sugar and another tablespoon of curaçao. Serves 8.

Lemon Mousse

1/2 cup lemon juice
1 cup sugar
4 eggs, separated
2 envelopes gelatin
1/2 cup cold water
3/4 cup boiling water
1/2 cup heavy cream
2 tablespoons grated lemon
   rind

Beat egg yolks and sugar together. Soften gelatin in cold water. Add boiling water and stir to dissolve. Mix in lemon juice. Pour half of the mixture into yolk and sugar mixture. Mix thoroughly and pour into remaining gelatin mixture. Stir and set aside. Whip cream and egg whites separately. Fold both into gelatin mixture. Turn into two-quart mold. Sprinkle lemon rind on top; chill until firm. Serves 8.

Strawberry Mousse

1 cup sliced strawberries
   (about 1/2 pint)
3 tablespoons sugar
3 tablespoons white creme de
   cacao
3/4 cup chilled heavy cream

In a small sauce pan combine the strawberries, the sugar, and 1 tablespoon of water, brir.g the mixture to a boil over moderately low heat, stirring, and cook it at a slow boil, stirring for 4 minutes.

Chill the mixture in a bowl, covered, for 1 to 2 hours, or until it is cold. In a food processor or blender purée the mixture, add the liqueur and transfer the purée to the bowl. In a chilled bowl beat the cream until it holds stiff peaks and fold it into the strawberry purée gently but thoroughly. Divide the mousse among stemmed dessert glasses and serve it immediately or chill it, covered, overnight. Serve with Devonshire cream to 4 persons.

Apricot Mousse

4 ounces dried apricots
2 tablespoons sugar
2 tablespoons cognac
1 cup chilled heavy cream

In a saucepan combine the apricots and 1 cup water, bring the water to a boil, and simmer the apricots, covered, for 15 to 20 minutes, or until they are soft. Add the sugar and simmer the mixture, mashing it with a spoon, for 3 to 5 minutes, or until thickened. Transfer mixture to a bowl, stir in the cognac, and chill the mixture, covered, for 1 to 2 hours, or until it is cold. In a chilled bowl beat the cream until it holds stiff peaks and fold it into the apricot mixture gently but thoroughly. Divide the mixture among stemmed dessert glasses and serve it immediately or chill it, covered, overnight. Serves 6.

Ginger Apple Mousse

1 1/2 teaspoons ground
   ginger
1 pound peeled McIntosh or
   Granny Smith apples,
   chopped
1 1/2 inch cube peeled
   gingerroot, sliced thin
2 tablespoons sugar, or to
   taste
1 teaspoon fresh lemon juice,
   or to taste
3/4 cup chilled heavy cream

In a saucepan combine the apples, the ginger, and 1/3 cup water, bring the liquid to a boil, and simmer the mixture, covered, stirring occasionally, until the apples are soft. Put the mixture into the food processor bowl; purée and add the sugar and lemon juice. Chill the mixture, covered, for 1 to 2 hours, or until it is cold. In a chilled bowl beat the cream to stiff peaks; fold it into the apple-ginger mixture gently but thoroughly. Divide among dessert glasses and serve it immediately or chill it, covered, overnight. Serves 4 to 6.

Banana Mousse

3/4 cup mashed ripe banana
  (about 2 bananas)
2 tablespoons firmly packed
  dark brown sugar
2 teaspoons fresh lemon
  juice, or to taste
3/4 cup chilled heavy cream

In a bowl mash together the banana, sugar, and lemon juice. In a chilled bowl beat the cream until it holds stiff peaks and fold it into the banana mixture gently but thoroughly. Divide the dessert among stemmed glasses. Top with additional cream, if you like, flavored with a pinch of nutmeg. Serves 4.

Prune Mousse

1 cup pitted prunes
1/2 cup Marsala wine
3-inch cinnamon stick
2 three-by-one-inch strips of
  fresh lemon rind
Sugar to taste
1 cup chilled heavy cream

In a saucepan combine the prunes, wine, cinnamon stick, rind, and 1/2 cup water, bring to a boil, and simmer, covered, for 20 minutes. Stir in sugar if you like, and simmer, uncovered, stirring occasionally for 5 minutes, or until it is thickened. Discard the cinnamon stick and rind and chill the mixture in a bowl, covered, for 1 to 2 hours, or until it is cold. In a food processor purée the mixture and transfer the purée to the bowl. In a chilled bowl beat the cream until it holds stiff peaks and fold it into the prune purée gently but thoroughly. Divide among dessert dishes; serve it immediately or chill it, covered, overnight. Serves 4 to 6.

Butter Cookies
Who can do without these?

1 cup butter
1 cup sugar
1 whole egg
1 extra egg yolk
1 teaspoon vanilla
Juice of one lemon
1 pound flour (about 4 cups)
Extra egg white for brushing
    tops of cookies, plus 1
    tablespoon water

Sift flour once before measuring and 3 times afterwards. Set aside. Cream butter and sugar. Add the whole egg and extra yolk, vanilla, and lemon juice. Add flour, just enough to roll the dough thin—about 4 cups.

Pinch off small amounts of dough and roll as thin as possible on a floured board with a floured rolling pin. Cut out with fancy cookie cutter or make into squares or rectangles with a pastry wheel. Place side by side on greased cookie tins or biscuit pan. Brush surface of each cookie with the extra egg white beaten slightly with a tabespoonful of water. Leave plain or sprinkle with the following topping:

2 tablespoons sugar
1 teaspoon cinnamon
2 tablespoons chopped almonds or
    pecans

To bake, place cookie tins in preheated moderate oven (375 degrees) and watch to see that they do not burn. Cook until golden-brown. These cookies keep indefinitely in an air-tight container.

Sidney wonders how long I will let an empty dish sit before a starving fellow.

Sponge Pudding

1 pint milk
1/2 cup butter
1 teaspoon vanilla
1 cup flour
4 egg yolks, well beaten
4 egg whites, well beaten

Put half of the milk in a bowl and place in another bowl or basin of hot water. Add melted butter, the flour made into a paste with the rest of the milk, and the egg yolks. Then, just before baking, fold in the well-beaten egg whites and the vanilla. Pour into pudding dish and set in a pan 1/4 full of hot water. Bake in a moderate oven (375 degrees) 45 minutes or until pudding sets. Serve with lemon sauce (see below).

Old-Fashioned Lemon Sauce

1/2 cup butter, softened but
    not melted
1 cup sugar
1 whole egg
Juice and grated rind of a
    lemon
1/4 cup boiling water

Cream butter with sugar. Add the egg and beat well.

Add boiling water, and beat again. Add the lemon juice and grated rind and stir well. Then pour into the top of a double boiler and set on the stove. Heat to the boiling point, stirring constantly. *Never let this sauce boil.* Serve at once, covering each portion of pudding with a generous amount of sauce.

Crumb Top Fruit Pudding

You can choose sliced peaches, rhubarb, sour cherries, huckleberries, blue-berries, strawberries, red or black raspberries or blackberries for this not-so-fattening foolproof pudding, good enough for company.

2 cups berries or sliced fruit
1/4 teaspoon cinnamon
1/2 cup sugar or to taste
1/4 cup butter
1/2 cup flour

Place the washed fruit into the bottom of a one-quart baking dish. Dust with cinnamon. Mix sugar, flour, and butter, then crumble it together with your fingers, like you do for a pie crust. Cover the fruit evenly with the crumbed mixture. Make 4 or 5 steam-escape holes and place pudding in 450-degree oven for 15 minutes. Reduce heat to 375 degrees for 20 to 30 minutes, or until fruit is cooked. Serve hot with whipped cream or vanilla ice cream. Serves 4.

Apple Crisp

6 tart apples
1 cup sugar
1/4 teaspoon ground cloves
1/2 teaspoon cinnamon
2 teaspoons lemon juice
3/4 cup sifted flour
1/8 teaspoon salt
6 tablespoons butter
1/4 cup chopped nut meats
Whipped cream or ice cream

Preheat oven to moderate (350 degrees).
Peel, core, and slice the apples into a bowl. Add one-half cup of the sugar, the spices and lemon juice. Mix lightly and pour into a buttered 2-quart casserole.
Blend the remaining sugar, flour, salt and butter to a crumbly consistency. Add the nuts and sprinkle over the apple mixture. Bake 45 minutes, or until the apples are tender and the crust is nicely browned. Serve with whipped cream or ice cream.

Cheese Pie

For the Crust:
1 1/2 cups Graham Cracker
   crumbs
2 tablespoons sugar
4 tablespoons butter, melted

For the Filling:
11 ounces cream cheese
   (room temperature)
2 eggs, well beaten
1 teaspoon vanilla
1/2 cup sugar
1 teaspoon Grand Marnier
   (more or less)

For the Topping:
1/4 cup sugar
1 pint sour cream

Preheat oven to 350 degrees.

For the crust, combine crumbs and 2 tablespoons sugar and butter. Make crust and bake 5 minutes. Cool.

For the filling, blend cream cheese on low speed. Add 1/2 beaten egg and beat until blended. Add the other 1/2 egg, continue beating. Gradually add 1/2 cup sugar, vanilla, and Grand Marnier. Pour into crust. Bake 20 minutes.

For the topping, spoon sour cream and 1/4 cup sugar together. Pour on top of pie. Turn oven off, put pie in oven for 4 minutes. Remove and refrigerate.

This pie is extremely rich, extremely satisfying, and extremely well liked by cats. And people.

Baked Custard with Caramel Sauce

1 cup cream
4 eggs
1 teaspoon vanilla
1 cup milk
1/3 cup white sugar
1/2 cup sugar (to caramelize)
Pinch of salt

Beat eggs until light and lemon-colored. Add sugar, dash of salt, vanilla, milk and cream, and mix well. Meanwhile, caramelize 1/2 cup sugar. Pour caramel into 6 individual custard cups or into 1 large baking dish and coat bottom and sides of dishes or dish. Pour the uncooked custard into this. Set in a pan 1/4 full of water and bake in moderate oven (375 degrees) until custard is set—about 30 minutes for the individual custards, 40 to 50 minutes for the large dish. Do not cook too long or it will become tough. Chill. Loosen edges of custard with a dull knife and turn individual custards out of molds, invert them on the dish on which they are to be served. Pour the caramel syrup over them.

Sherry Custard

6 eggs, separated
2/3 cup sugar
3/4 cup sherry
1/4 teaspoon salt
Strawberries as garnish

Mix the egg yolks and sugar in the top of 1 1/2 quart double boiler. Set over simmering (never boiling) water and beat with an electric beater until fluffy.

Add the sherry gradually and continue beating until the mixture resembles whipped cream. Cool quickly and chill.

Before serving, beat the egg whites with the salt until stiff. Fold into the chilled custard and turn into a glass serving dish. Serve garnished with strawberries.

Bananas Caribbean

4 medium bananas
1/4 cup brown sugar, packed
1/2 cup fresh orange juice
1/4 teaspoon nutmeg
1/4 teaspoon cinnamon
1/2 cup sherry
1 tablespoon butter
2 tablespoons light rum

Preheat oven to hot (450 degrees).

Peel the bananas and split them in half lengthwise. Place in a buttered 10 x 6 x 2-inch baking dish.

Combine the brown sugar with the orange juice, spices and sherry. Heat and pour over the bananas. Dot with butter. Bake 10 to 15 minutes, until bananas are tender, basting once or twice. When finished, remove from oven; sprinkle with rum.

Baked Bananas and White Grapes

4 bananas
1/4 cup sugar
1/8 teaspoon salt
1/2 lemon, juice and rind
1 teaspoon cinnamon
1/4 teaspoon nutmeg
2 tablespoons butter
4 tablespoons maple syrup
1/2 cup seedless white grapes

Slice peeled bananas lengthwise and crosswise. Place a layer in the bottom of a baking dish. Add a few grapes. Sprinkle with some of the sugar and spices. Add the remainder of the bananas in another layer, then the rest of the grapes and more sugar and spices. Dot with butter, add salt, pour syrup over mixture and add the thinly sliced lemon. Bake in a moderate oven (375 degrees) for 20 minutes.

Brown sugar may be substituted for maple syrup in which case add 1 tablespoon of water before baking. Serves 4.

White Grapes and Sour Cream

1 pound white grapes,
  removed from stem,
  washed, and picked over
1 cup dark brown sugar
1 1/2 cups sour cream
1/4 cup dark rum

Mix grapes with sugar so every grape is covered. Use a 4-ounce white porcelain, oven-proof ramikins to heat and serve this dessert. Arrange 2 heaping tablespoons of grapes in the bottom of each ramikin. Mix rum with sour cream and heap rum and sour cream mixture on grapes to top of ramikin. Place ramikins on cookie sheet; when ready to serve, place under heated broiler for 3 minutes or until bubbly brown. Serve immediately. Looks classy, tastes great and takes about five minutes to prepare. Toss the cats a few grapes to divert them from the cream.

To adapt this recipe for summer serving, mix all the ingredients together in a serving bowl. Cover and refrigerate over night. Take to a picnic or serve in chilled glass bowls at the end of a summer supper by candlelight.

Apricots à la Cognac

1 pound dried apricots
2/3 cup sugar
Cognac to cover

Combine all the ingredients and let stand at least twenty-four hours. The flavor is improved if the fruit is allowed to steep in cognac for more than a week. Serve chilled, with whipped cream. Serves 6.

Cherries Jubilee

1 can pitted black cherries
1 tablespoon sugar
1 tablespoon cornstarch
1/4 cup warmed kirsch or
   cognac
Vanilla ice cream

Drain the cherries, reserving the juice.

Mix the sugar with the cornstarch and add one cup of the reserved juice, a little at a time. Cook three minutes, stirring constantly. Add the cherries and pour the kirsch over the top. Ignite the kirsch and ladle the sauce over the cherries.

Serve over vanilla ice cream. Serves 6.

NOTE ON SAUCES

How to Make Fresh Tomato Sauce:
Nowadays I don't like anything but fresh tomato sauce, but for years I made spaghetti sauce only with tomato paste and canned plum tomatoes and cooked it forever. "Slow simmer it for hours or all day" was always the advice from cookbooks and good Italian cooks I knew. When I first discovered small cans of pesto on the back shelf in Murray's cheese store in Greenwich Village, I knew that old way of saucing pasta had ended for me.

But during the ripe tomato richness of August and September in the Hudson Valley I developed a yen for fresh tomato sauce, and this is how I do it now:

2 pounds fresh ripe tomatoes (the Italian plum variety are good but not essential)
4 tablespoons olive oil
1 medium onion or 4 scallions (well cleaned with about three inches of green left on) chopped fine
1 bay leaf
3 fresh basil leaves
2 cloves garlic, mashed and chopped fine

Chop the tomatoes coarsely in the food processor; remove from bowl and set aside. Then chop the onions or slice the scallions with the fine slicing disk. Simmer the onions in the olive oil until they are just golden, add the garlic and stir around until it cooks through. Add the tomatoes and the bay leaf. Season to taste, add a little pinch of sugar—it makes quite a difference.

Simmer and stir occasionally with a wooden spoon until the sauce is reduced and not watery. Add basil strips. You should have 3 to 4 cups of sauce. You can freeze this or keep it in the refrigerator for 4 or 5 days. As my former neighbors on Sullivan Street used to say, "Good to keep at the ready if you like to cook Italian."

How to Make Bechamel Sauce:

This is the first sauce we were taught to make in my foods class at Langley High School. And my mentor, Craig Claiborne (he doesn't know he is, but by now you should), says, "If a home cook could learn to make one sauce, this would be the most valuable. It is the basis for countless dishes."

2 tablespoons flour
2 tablespoons butter
1 cup milk
Pinch of salt, freshly ground
   black pepper
Pinch of freshly grated
   nutmeg

Melt butter in saucepan; don't let it brown. Add flour, stir with whisk and blend well. Let cook, stirring all the while, for five minutes. In a separate pan, heat milk almost to boiling. Stir flour and butter while adding hot milk. Keep stirring until mixture bubbles. It will be thickened by then. Simmer for about 5 minutes and season to taste.

This recipe makes one cup of sauce. Double, triple, even sextuple it for more, depending on your need. To make thinner sauce, use 1 tablespoon of butter and 1 of flour to 1 cup milk; to make thicker, use 3 tablespoons of butter and 3 of flour to 1 cup of milk.

You can add cheese to this basic sauce and stir over low heat until melted. Season with anything from Dijon mustard to Tabasco to your taste.

When you find a recipe that calls for velouté, it just means to substitute broth for the milk—either chicken, fish or beef broth. And now that fresh herbs are widely available (thank heavens—dried herbs are not as good, but they *are* stronger so use half as much as the fresh) you can just add 1 tablespoon of freshly chopped dill or parsley or basil or all three to the basic white sauce and have an extravagantly delicious sauce for fish or omelets or whatever arouses your appetite.

For complete details on lots of other sauces, I suggest you turn to *The Original New York Times Cookbook*. You'll find 15 pages of sauces and special butter mixtures there. I keep referring to that book because I learned so much about the universe of foods from it when I was given my first copy in 1965. The back finally fell off that edition and in 1981 some other dear

friends gave me a new copy that I use frequently, along with information and inspiration from my other favorite cooking teachers: Alice B. Toklas, Julia Childs, Nancy Hanst, Decker Johnson, John Bodnar, James Beard, Terence John Murphy, Aunt Rose, my brother, George Wilson Morin, Sharon Clancy Lienau, Aunt Biz, Peter Wesley-Burke, Joseph Moody, my sister, Dr. Eleanor Morin Davis, my daughter, my son, and another wonderful book, *The Renaissance Cookbook*, which gives some new insights into the history and scope of the human appetite, if not the feline one.

Here's some good information to have if you like to cook and love to eat. How many times have you wondered what the following terms mean when you've seen them on menus or read about them in food columns?

Each sauce or cuisine is followed by the required ingredients, but not the quantity.

A l'Americaine (lobster or shrimp): Butter, onion, a little garlic, white wine, cognac, reduction of tomatoes, tarragon, bay leaf, parsley

Alla Puttanesca: Olive oil, garlic, anchovies, black olives, capers, tomato sauce, stock, parsley

Armenian (lamb or beef): Butter, onion, garlic, stock, reduction of tomatoes, paprika, allspice or cinnamon, black pepper, parsley

Chinese (shellfish): Peanut oil, ginger, garlic, sake or sherry, catsup, soy sauce, stock, scallions, coriander leaves

Creole (meat): Olive oil, garlic, onion, green pepper, chopped green olives, tomato sauce, brown stock, thyme, parsley

Greek (broiled fish): Olive oil, sliced onion, sliced fresh tomatoes, white wine or ouzo, fennel, oregano, black pepper

Marinara: Olive oil, garlic, reduction of tomatoes, parsley

Milanese: Olive oil, garlic, anchovy, white wine tomato sauce, dill

Niçoise (seafood): Olive oil, garlic, anchovies, white wine, reduction of tomatoes, capers, lemon slices, black pepper

Pan Roast (shellfish): Butter, chili sauce, Worcestershire sauce, lemon juice, cream, celery salt, paprika

Pizzaluoia (meat): Olive oil, garlic, anchovies, parsley, black and green olives, white wine, brown stock, tomatoes, black pepper

Spanish: Olive oil, onion, garlic, reduction of tomatoes, parsley

ACKNOWLEDGMENTS

Books I have read, studied, and been inspired by in all the time I have been cooking, and particularly in the last months while I've been putting this book together are hereby gratefully acknowledged.

Out of Kentucky, by Marion Flexner;

The American Gothic Cookbook, compiled by Joan Liffring-Zug;

The Boston Cooking School Cook Book, 1925 edition, by Fannie Merritt Farmer;

Pennsylvania Dutch Cook Book of Fine Old Recipes;

Pasta Cookery, by Sophie Kay;

The Cheese Book, by Vivian Marquis and Patricia Haskell;

Cooking Ideas from Villa d'Este, by Jean Govoni Salvadore;

Better Homes and Gardens' Golden Treasury of Cooking;

Come for Cocktails, Stay for Supper, by Marian Burros and Lois Levine;

Joy of Cooking, by Irma S. Rombauer and Marion Rombauer Becker (1980 edition);

Julia Child and More Company, by Julia Child;

Mastering the Art of French Cooking, vol. 2, by Julia Child with Simone Beck;

Modern Encyclopedia of Cooking, vol. 2, by Meta Given;

The Alice B. Toklas Cookbook, by Alice B. Toklas;

The Provincetown Seafood Cookbook, by Howard Mitcham;

The Good Food, by Daniel Halpern and Julie Strand;

The Renaissance Cookbook, by Berengario delle Cinqueterre;

and as mentioned on other pages of this book,

The Original New York Times Cook Book, by Craig Claiborne.